Joy Through a Wardrobe

The Chronicles' Companion

The Chronicles' Companion is a series of poetic and devotional-style reflections on C.S. Lewis's *The Chronicles of Narnia*. Through dynamic poetry and challenging reflections, *The Chronicles' Companion* series uncovers the captivating, hidden element in Lewis's classic tales so that you, the reader, can better grasp each Chronicles' spiritual insights. This series will provide a *Companion* to pair with each *Chronicle*.

Whether you have read one or all seven stories that comprise Lewis's Narniad, your reading doubtless enthralled you with a fantastic sense of wonder that permeated your imagination, page after page. There is a reason for your enchantment that goes beyond good prose and well-used literary techniques. Each *Chronicle* is shaped by and exudes a certain hidden air that buries itself deep in its reader's mind. But what is this air, this hidden contagion? *The Chronicles' Companion* series endeavors to remedy this riddle via meter, rhyme, and contemplation.

Joy Through a Wardrobe
The Chronicles' Companion Series

By Donald W. Catchings Jr.

RESOURCE *Publications* • Eugene, Oregon

JOY THROUGH A WARDROBE

The Chronicles' Companion Series

Copyright © 2020 Donald W. Catchings Jr. All rights reserved. Except for brief quotations in critical publications or reviews, no part of this book may be reproduced in any manner without prior written permission from the publisher. Write: Permissions, Wipf and Stock Publishers, 199 W. 8th Ave., Suite 3, Eugene, OR 97401.

Resource Publications
An Imprint of Wipf and Stock Publishers
199 W. 8th Ave., Suite 3
Eugene, OR 97401

www.wipfandstock.com

PAPERBACK ISBN: 978-1-7252-5342-1
HARDCOVER ISBN: 978-1-7252-5343-8
EBOOK ISBN: 978-1-7252-5344-5

Manufactured in the U.S.A.   01/13/20

For Harper and Hannah
May you find Joy

But many of the priests and Levites and chief of the fathers, who were ancient men, that had seen the first house, when the foundation of this house was laid before their eyes, wept with a loud voice; and many shouted aloud for joy.

—Ezra 3:12, KJV

Contents

Preface | ix
Introduction: Enjoying the Wardrobe | xi

1. Finding Good Fortune | 1
2. Tea-Time Deceit | 8
3. Winter-Wandering and Woe | 14
4. A Disastrous Delight | 21
5. Of Others' Worlds | 28
6. Certainly Surprised | 34
7. A Helping Hand | 40
8. Not Safe, but Safety | 46
9. COLD, COLD, COLD | 52
10. A New Day Dawning | 57
11. Sweetly Growing Guilt | 63
12. Lion-Hearted Lad | 69
13. Wintery-Woes Mended | 75
14. Guilt, Fortunately Forgiven | 82
15. Romp . . . Roll . . . Rejoice | 88
16. Heroic Helm of Nations | 94
17. Returning with Wishful Wonder | 100

Epilogue: Joy Through a Wardrobe | 108

Preface

When I began this endeavor, I was not quite sure where the work would lead. I knew I wanted to write poetry concerning the hidden element in C.S. Lewis's *The Lion, the Witch and the Wardrobe*, an insight that has been of great importance to me. (Thank you, Dr. Ward.) Still, I did not know who the work was for: young teens? adults? Who would want to read something so esoteric (the initiated few)? At first, I tried to think too academically. Then, I realized that would only further limit the influence of a unique endeavor that I want to be enjoyed by as wide an audience as possible. Then again, I knew that a good work of literature must be focused. So who would the work be made for? Eventually, I realized that I could not focus on the who; I had to focus on the what—what this work could provide to those seeking a clearer path through the Narnian woods and those who want to relish a little while longer in Narnia's joyful journey.

Don't get me wrong; this book is not meant to enhance on Lewis's work—that would be a foolish attempt (verging on blasphemy). Nor is this work an attempt at kindly suggesting that you have misunderstood this first *Chronicle*, or that you have read it wrong all along. I merely want to help you realize that there may be more to it than you have yet grasped. It is my desire that this book will help remove those unrealized shadows that, unbeknownst to you, may have hindered the full beam of Lewis's jovial intent. This book is meant to be read alongside *The Lion, the Witch and the Wardrobe* so that it may help you align your eyes with the light of Lewis's penmanship.

Whether you are a parent who is reading through the Narniad with your children, a teenager who is picking up *The Lion* for the first time, or one of those people who is now old enough to read fairytales again, this book is a great companion to accompany you on your journey. I have crafted the poems that they may guide you along the path of joy in Lewis' *The Lion*. With each chapter, there will be three poems which usually deal with the beginning, middle, and end of their respective chapter. Just as you should read Lewis's work attentively, I suggest that these poems be read attentively. Above all, may you Enjoy them in the fullest. As for the reflections, there is a single reflection that concludes each chapter. However, the reflections are not meant to merely summarize Lewis's own chapter or the poems I have written. I have shaped them so that they may help lead you along the path of reinstating joy's lordship in your own life. Again, above all, may you Enjoy them to the fullest.

Now it is time to set off on your journey to find joy through a wardrobe.

Introduction

Enjoying the Wardrobe

Since *The Lion, the Witch and the Wardrobe* was first published in 1950, C. S. Lewis's fairy-tale series, *The Chronicles of Narnia*, has been the refuge for myriad hopeful runaways seeking freedom and asylum under the guard of Cair Paravel, adventure in the Wild Wastelands of the North, and solace adrift the sea of white lilies. It is "Narnia and the North!" or "For Aslan!" that has been the cry of such hopeful hearts and minds: children as well as adults, students as well as scholars, even those on-the-fence of belief, as well as the dedicated Christian. And since you have decided to peer into the pages of this book, I am sure what I speak of is hitting home right now. You are likely recalling your favorite moments from the Narniad (as the series is sometimes called): a moment which causes a tingle of joy to run up your spine; a scene that sends a jolt of excitement to clench your fist tight; opening words that fashion a grin from ear to ear; a conclusion that releases a sigh of relief to ease your weary mind. Or maybe thinking on Lewis's fairy-tale series causes something truly beyond expression, something so beyond words as to be secret.

Many have wondered why Lewis's Narniad is so drawing. This wonder has caused more than a few to search for the inner fabric which pulls *The Chronicles* together and continually beckons its reader to bask in the wonderment of another world full of excitement. Is it the adventures? Is it the relatable or fun characters? Is it the powerful presence of Aslan? Yes and no. These are part of the reason you go back again and again into that wardrobe. But there is something more that takes each of these threads and seams them together. Again, many have tried to figure out what

INTRODUCTION

this is—to know what Lewis harnessed; to understand how Lewis created this world.

Of those who have sought to uncover this secret and put it to paper, I think one has been successful—Michael Ward in his work, *Planet Narnia*. In *Planet Narnia*, Michael Ward uncovers what actually has made the Narniad so appealing to such a varied audience for over six decades, and why the true cohesive element escaped the grasp of most critics and fans alike throughout this time. Apparently the secret code undergirding Lewis's Narniad is a dual-faceted theory best described with the complicated term pre-Copernican donegality—meaning, for each of the seven planets in the pre-Copernican cosmos, there is a correlating chronicle of Narnia whose theme, plot, motifs, etc. are governed by that planet's influence. (Precisely what this means will be explained in due time.) Furthermore, Ward reveals that Lewis developed the Narniad as a fairytale that draws the reader to look along the light of the seven planets' influence.

Not many reading this will have any clue what looking along the light of a planet means, nor what the pre-Copernican cosmos is, let alone what the light of a pre-Copernican planet is. Such knowledge is not necessary to love or properly Enjoy Lewis's work; in fact, it can get in the way. The reader is not supposed to see pre-Copernican cosmological light when reading any of *The Chronicles of Narnia*; the light is supposed to be hidden. Not hidden in such a way that the reader is to look for it. Hidden like the sun at noon; whether or not the sun is there never crosses your mind. At noonday, you are too busy looking at the world that is clearly seen by the sun's light to consider how you are seeing it. For most of our lives, the sun is, in this way, hidden. When you walk around during the daytime, under the unseen influence of the sun, and are able to observe the world around you, Lewis would consider you to be looking along the light of the sun. Lewis called this, via another's work (Samuel Alexander's *Space, Time, and Deity*), "Enjoyment."[1]

---

1. C. S. Lewis, *Surprised by Joy: The Shape of My Early Life* (San Francisco: HarperOne, 2017), 265.

INTRODUCTION

What does it mean to Enjoy a story?

Lewis believed there to be two different ways of experiencing things: you can Contemplate, or you can Enjoy—you can look at or look along. Lewis wrote an essay that explained this thought more clearly than I can in his essay "Meditation in a Toolshed." I suggest that this essay be read if you want to be able to fully understand Lewis's thoughts on how a story is meant to be read. However, for the sake of time, I am here going to provide a short rendition of the imagery he employed in his essay:

> Imagine you have foolishly locked yourself in a wardrobe. While standing in this darkened wardrobe, you look down and see a beam of light shining through the key whole—you are Contemplating that beam of light. Then imagine that you bend down and peer through the keyhole which the light is shining through. Your eyes begin to adjust to the light. First, you see the room outside; then, the little details of the room become clear—the ridges in the wooden floor, the ceiling's texture, the dust particles floating in front of the window on the exterior wall, and so on. Finally, your eyes adjust so that you are able to look beyond the room, out the window. The world outside the room becomes clear (trees, houses, lawnmowers, etc.). You are Enjoying that beam of light shining through the keyhole.

This applies very nicely to writing and reading fiction novels. When you look at a story via the light of your own perspective, you are Contemplating that story. When you look along a story from the perspective the author draws for you, you are Enjoying that story.

Let me further clarify the idea of Contemplation and Enjoyment with another example. As Lewis uses the word, Contemplation is looking at something through the lenses of something else; you are always Enjoying the lenses you are looking through and Contemplating the thing you are looking at. Example: Looking at Greek myths from the perspective of the Christian faith is Contemplation—you cannot help but Contemplate a worldview that

INTRODUCTION

you do not live by. And this Contemplation can only take place while you are Enjoying another worldview. As I am a Christian, I look at everything via the beam of Christianity. I Enjoy Christianity and, by the Enjoyment of Christianity, I see the rest of the world as God, in Christ, means it to be seen.

When you are reading *The Lion, the Witch and the Wardrobe*, you are not supposed to be Contemplating the story; you are supposed to be Enjoying the story. It is on the author to draw the eye of the reader into the story; however, it is up to the reader to cast off those outside influences that keep drawing their minds out of the book in order to Contemplate (look at) the book. Lewis has crafted the Narniad to be looked along, not looked at. Lewis has created a specific air, spirit, and influence that governs each Chronicle. He has set a certain light in motion within the pages of each story. The reader is not meant to see it or look for it. The reader is meant to look along it, to feel it, to let it weave together in their mind, to be captivated by its beauty, to be overcome by its influence. Yet in this work, ironically enough, I am endeavoring to take that air, that spirit, that fabric which runs through *The Lion The Witch and The Wardrobe* and shine a light on it so that what is meant to be Enjoyed can be Contemplated.

As Ward has a good, justifiable reason for uncovering the secret element in Lewis's Narniad, I have a good, justifiable reason for doing the same—albeit in a less academic manner. In this work, I am not advancing on Ward's theory; I am merely attempting to open the wardrobe door in a different way, using poetry and reflection to allow the reader to see the pre-Copernican spiritual symbols that influence, specifically, *The Lion, the Witch and the Wardrobe*: the spiritual symbols of Jupiter. Overall, the justifiable reason for doing this, though I know Lewis painstakingly left the secret covered and believed it should not be known, is because too many have tried to Contemplate the Narniad incompletely. In seeking out that hidden element, many have Contemplated the stories from an incomplete light. I cannot say that those who have guessed at other underlying elements in each Chronicle, especially biblical ones, have not seen something that is real—i.e. the sacrifice of Aslan on Edmund's behalf mirroring the crucifixion of Christ. But, I can say that this is only a part of the light. Such a sacrifice is only one element of the spirit that influences *The Lion, the Witch and The Wardrobe*. I believe revealing that secret element that guides the theme, plot, and motifs of Lewis's first Chronicle will ironically enough draw a reader's eyes back to look along the light they were never meant to see. After Contemplating the story for a little while, the reader will be able to truly Enjoy *The Lion, the Witch and the Wardrobe*, in every sense of the word.

What is a pre-Copernican cosmological spiritual symbol?

Now to at least basically understand what a pre-Copernican cosmological spiritual symbol is. In the medieval world, before Kepler and Copernicus, it was believed that the planets—seven known other than Earth at the time (a special number in the ancient and medieval mind)—revolved around the Earth: the Moon, Mercury, Venus, the Sun, Mars, Jupiter, and Saturn. Moreover, there was not a seemingly endless universe beyond what we know today as our solar system; there was an enclosed system known as the cosmos: the seven planets and the stars encased within the *Primum Mobile*. That was it.

The Medieval mind believed that each of these planets had a list of characteristics that defined them, and they were endowed with and exuded certain spiritual influences on the Earth. To put it lightly, as a scholar of Medieval Literature, Lewis felt a special connection to this Medieval view of the cosmos. As Ward reveals, much of Lewis's writing revolves around the influence of the planets. Therefore, for any reader of Medieval texts or texts written under the influence of Medieval minds (like *The Chronicles of Narnia*), the characteristics that were attributed to the seven planets remain important. However, for brevity's sake, I am only going to unveil the most central characteristics of Jupiter and Saturn, for it is Jupiter and Saturn which guided

Lewis's development of plot, imagery, motifs, and other literary techniques in the first Chronicle.[2]

Jupiter is *Fortuna Major* (the greater fortune). In the Medieval world, this planet represented, in a word, chivalry—a code of conduct that calls for bravery in battle, honor in court, and gentleness at home. According to Ward, it is Jupiter's influence that governs *The Lion, the Witch and the Wardrobe*. Of the many characteristics that are part of Jupiter's chivalry, I think there are two that summarize it well and are most central in this Chronicle. Maybe once I state it, it will be a little obvious; I believe that these Jovial (Jupiter) characteristics are lion-heartedness and laughter.

The entire story revolves around characters who must choose to do the right thing no matter the cost. This is lion-heartedness at its finest. In all the great stories of kings, knights, and damsels in distress, the hero's lion-heartedness is what brings joy to the reader's heart, soul, and mind. It is for such joy (jovialness) that readers return to the tales of men like Arthur and Aragorn. Moreover, it is the lion-heartedness in this story that leads, in the end, to laughter—the most agreed upon sign of joy. And laughter, I think, is the other defining Jovial characteristic in this story because in it the reader realizes that courage has reaped its reward.

Saturn, on the other hand, is not represented positively in this Chronicle, nor are many of its characteristics understood in a positive way in the Medieval world. Saturn is *Infortuna Major* (the least fortunate). The Saturnine characteristic which seems to be most central in this Chronicle is envy. Not only is Edmund envious of Peter, the Witch envies Aslan. Neither the Witch nor Edmund have the right to rule in the same manner as the one they envy: they do not have their power; they cannot take their place; they cannot step out from under their authority. Both are overcome with this most self-destructive of banes, the overwhelming Saturnine characteristic of envy. Edmund and the Witch are not alone in this weakness. In all those stories of great knights and

---

[2]. Here it must be suggested that Lewis' poem "The Planets" be read. It is in this poem that Lewis maps out the characteristics of each planet in the pre-Copernican cosmos.

kings, we cannot forget the envious villains. We must not forget the Saturnine enemies, Mordred and Morgoth.

After discovering that the Earth is not the center of our solar system, the Medieval view of the cosmos faded into a bleak and vast universe; the ideas concerning the planets' spiritual influences dissolved with the scientifically incomplete view of the heavens. As a scholar of Medieval Literature, Lewis felt the loss of the planets' spiritual influence on Earth to be detrimental. Lewis knew good and well that the Earth was not the center of our solar system. Lewis knew good and well that there were more than seven planets. Still, as a lover of Medieval Literature, he also knew that when the world of literature lost its ground for employing the spiritual symbols of the planets in art, it lost a valuable symbol that artists could use to display the moral law inherent in mankind.

Reading *The Lion*

As you read through *The Lion, the Witch and the Wardrobe*, as well as this companion, remember that every word and every scene was shaped by Lewis so that the reader would look along the battle between Jove (Jupiter) and Saturn. Lewis painted each conflict so that the reader could take the long journey with each character from incomplete to complete Joy. Try not to focus on biblical allusions or other images that pull your mind from the work at hand. They are there, and they are beautiful. But they will not give you the full picture. For now, until you can truly see Jove's light, try to do what is not meant to be done, Contemplate Jove's influence. Once you have come to understand what Lewis has done with imagery, then you will be able to properly read, Enjoy, *The Chronicles*. I am afraid this cannot be done without understanding (at least basically) the characteristics of the seven planets. This is why I must suggest that you read Lewis's own work on the subject ("Meditations in a Toolshed" and "The Planets"), as well as Ward's *Planet Narnia*.

Ward suggests—I believe he is right—that Lewis wanted to reinsert the planets' influence into society. Lewis wanted each planet's moral influence to make its way back into the hearts and minds of mankind. What better way to do this than draw the hearts and minds of children to look along the courage of Jupiter? What better way to do this than bring the youth of a nation to stand against the dark wiles of Saturn? It is no wonder that Lewis used four kids to liberate Narnia and to draw his readers into his task of reinstating the character of Jove—laughter, courage, forgiveness, justness, gentleness, celebration—into their imagination and world. As God uses the praise of babes as a stronghold that silences His enemies, Lewis uses the imagination of the young (at least young at heart) to build a fortress of Joy against a hundred years of winter.[3]

(To understand a summarized version of Lewis' thoughts on each planet's spiritual influence, one must read his poem "The Planets.")

---

3. Ps 8:2 KJV.

1
Finding Good Fortune

Finding Good Fortune

By Jove I must say,
I believe that today
Fortune has smiled on us.

By Jove we have found
Freedom in this house.
Fortune has smiled on us.

By Jove that old chap,
He won't care a snap.
Fortune has smiled on us.

By Jove in this country,
Adventure aplenty,
Fortune has smiled on us.

By Jove, ventures wait
With break of day.
Fortune has smiled on us.

Making the Best of it

Sometimes rain falls
And blinds your eyes.
Sometimes plans change;
But, no need to grumble.
When the rain falls,
Adjust your eyes.
When the plans change,
Sift through the rubble
    Of the unexplored world
    That surrounds you;
    The hidden worlds around you.
Just round the corner,
You never know,
Adventure waits,
You just have to go.
Peak round the corner
And you will know
Surprise awaits,
Wherever you go . . .
    There will always be
    A chance of rain.
    Take a chance; go and play.
Run up the stairs.
Slide down the hall.
Expect new secrets
Behind each door.
Glide down the stairs.
Creep through the hall.
You'll find secrets,
That is for sure.

There is adventure,
If only you look
In a nook or open a book.
Maybe you might,
If in the mode,
Peak into that
Old Wardrobe.
And if you might
Go peak and probe,
Peer into that
Old Wardrobe,
    Just remember to
    Leave the door cracked
    If you want to get back.

A Meeting of Friends

Crunch-crunch. Under my feet.
Crunch-crunch. Mystery.
The cold, the night, the lamp-post light:
A strange new wood—winter delight.

Crunch-crunch. Over the snow.
Crunch-crunch. I do go.
I hear the sound of little feet:
In this dark wood, who can it be?

Pitter. A friend or foe?
Patter. I don't know!
Half goat, half man with reddish face:
A shocking sight in this new place.

Pitter. A Christmas gift?
Patter. Snowy sift.
An Umbrella over his head;
A red muffler around his neck.

O' my. A goodly faun.
O' me. Little girl.
At last she's come, Daughter of Eve—
Goodness gracious, O' Goodness me.
Crunch-crunch.

Learning to Look Along Fortune

C.S. Lewis begins his series, *The Chronicles of Narnia*, with a scene, chapter, and entire novel filled with childlike trust in fortune. It must be stated here that childlike trust is not a negative thing. Childlike trust is something our world could use a lot more of. You see, while the surrounding world screams, 'You are not fortunate!—There is no reason to romp and revel in joy or jubilee!', or while the devil on your shoulder whispers, 'What reason could you possibly have for being merry and mirthful?', the hopefulness of youth says, 'Even when good has gone out the window and fortune seems to have faded with fairytales, good fortune can be found.' It is this kind of childlike trust that Lewis brings to life in *The Lion, the Witch and the Wardrobe*. It is this kind of childlike trust that is meant to revitalize our imagination, resurrect in us a childlike hope, help us find good fortune in unfortunate circumstances, and lead us to look along the light of Joy.

Children are often thought to bicker and bemoan the silliest things; yet, Lewis shows that children tend to find light where there does not seem to be any and hope when good logic says that there is none. No matter how irreverent adults may consider it, children find a way to make light of heavy situations. Lewis is trying to remind us that those who have childlike hope see wonders, adventure, or fortune when everyone else sees despair.

In the joyful mind of children, a makeshift fort becomes a grand fortress; a broom becomes a noble steed; a large house becomes the subject of a vast exploration party. Lewis is trying to tell us that it is in the imagination of children that hope lies, and this hope is not a lie. It is imagination that leads to unexplored worlds, uncharted islands, and unknown frontiers. It is on these imaginative fronts that young people are able to test the waters of courage or cowardice. Here they have a chance to be the hero: to confront evil witches, race against impossible odds, rescue a traitor, or tuck-tail and run home.

In the world of imagination, we can test what kind of person we really are. Lewis is calling us—the world at large—to be like these four. Look past the rainy day that canceled our plans—make the best of it. Seek adventure in our misfortune and find that we can make it fortune. Here, in our imagination, we can resurrect the joy and wonder of youth; we can once again allow ourselves to peak and peer into the mysterious Wardrobe. But take heed. What was at first only the testing of imagination will soon turn into a real test of heart, mind, soul, and strength. In this real test, courage is still required, and the cost is more than imagined—as comes to play in the closing of chapter one when Lucy meets Mr. Tumnus.

Lewis has done something great here. He has taken a situation which seems most peculiar—surely silly, strange, and even frightening for an adult—and created a merry air of intrigue that leads the reader past the scene's peculiarity. Rather than feeling the dangerous suspense that should accompany finding a frozen wood, country, or possibly world at the back of a wardrobe, the reader is pulled into this tundra by the gentle, snow-laden curiosity of a little girl. Though this place is quite queer, the joyful air gives assurance that everything will be okay and readies the reader for the lighthearted meeting under the lamp-post.

Lucy should be losing her mind. Logic says she has already lost it. But, because children are quite naturally curious, and in their curiosity seem to give fortune the benefit of the doubt, Lucy is calmly overwhelmed with the joy of wonder. The confounding sight of a faun clad with red muffler, holding an umbrella, and carrying what looks to be Christmas packages, appears in the light of a lamp-post which is shining in the middle of a wood, does not deter this young mind.

What about you? When you come across an unexpected situation, do you meet it with fear or wonder? What would govern your reaction in such a strange, silly, and even frightening situation: faith in fortune or mistrust in chance?

No matter how you may answer such questions, it seems that Lewis is trying to call us—his readers—to consider or reconsider how we see our world. Rather than looking at our world like an outsider, observing and critiquing the misfortune which surrounds us, Lewis is calling us to look along the light of fortune in our lives so that we may see Goodness itself is that beam which we are ever journeying toward, and even through war, rain, and snow is illuminating our whole world. I think he is suggesting, and I agree with him, that we must re-learn to hope like children: we must remember how to find and follow good fortune in desperate situations. Then we can rejoice in all things. Then we can, like the four Pevensie siblings, make the best of it.

2

Tea-Time Deceit

Tea-Time Deceit

Come with me. Come with me; you can't be alone.
We can have tea in my humble home.
It is not far, just down the road.

> *I will go. I will go, my dear friendly Faun.*
> *But I tell you now, I shan't stay long.*
> *My family will wonder where I have gone.*

Take my arm. Take my arm and we will go.
My umbrella will ward off the snow
And soon my fire will melt off the cold.

Come on in. Come on in there's plenty of room.
Take a seat right here; kick back for a few,
Where Spring's red flower is never in bloom.

> *Many thanks. Many thanks. What a lovely cave.*
> *The books, the fire, it's cozy and safe.*
> *I really love what you've done with the place.*

O' I wish . . . How I wish you could have seen
How wonderful and lovely this land used to be,
When joy came alive and danced through the trees.

Relax now. Relax now. I'll play you a tune.
Sit back. Sip your tea as I uncase my flute.
No need to worry, you'll be off soon.

Betrayal or Bravery

You do not see what I must do.
I must give you up, betray you—
Our friendship can never reign,
                        Eternally.
You cannot see that I am in league
With the Winter's only White Queen.
The one through who winter does reign
                        Eternally.
Please forgive me my dear little friend.
She's not the real Queen of this cold land,
But her will rules and her wickedness reigns
                        Eternally.
All of my life has been filled with strife.
These hills were once teeming with life.
Yet in my short days, death seems to reign
                        Eternally.
I'll give you up; it's what I must do.
I have no choice, but to betray you.
If I don't, over my flesh, stone will reign
                        Eternally.

Oh my dear, sweet friendly faun,
You do not have to be evil's pawn.
You must not let winter, over you, reign
                        Eternally.
Will you let sorrow turn you from truth?
It is your choice: what will you do?
Will you let betrayal or bravery reign
                        Eternally?

The Beginning of Friendship

A puddle of woe drenching the floor;
A wet handkerchief soaked with guilt;
A sorrowful heart blubbering away;
There's only one way to wipe tears away.

The kind concern of heartfelt rapport—
The place where friendship is firmly built;
The loving ear that listens away;
This is the way to wipe tears away.

The passing of tears will bring hard truth—
A truth of guilt still being made,
While the guilty explains guilt away;
There's only one way to melt guilt away.

A gracious hand that mends hard truth
With childlike forgiveness, without debt paid—
The courage to cast the treason away—
This is the way to melt guilt away.

The Sure Foundation of Friendship and Forgiveness

Both friendship and forgiveness are among the most challenging obstacles in life's journey; and yet, they are pivotal to living a content and cheerful life. What complicates things further is the fact that, at some point, most friendships hinge on forgiveness and sometimes even begin in it—this is one of those points.

To combat the cold road of condemnation that is too often chosen, Lewis has placed two Jovial characters on cross-paths: the red-clad faun who happens to meet the faithful, fortunate, and forgiving little girl from another world. As he confesses, Mr. Tumnus has secretly agreed to kidnap a human if he should ever find one. When he realizes she is innocent, helpless, and kind, he must repent. In Lewis's world, the radiant looking faun must not betray the gentle, festal, and helpless little girl; but, it is just as important that the little girl forgive the faun, for this is also Jovial—in this, she exhibits the foundational characteristic of *The Lion, the Witch and the Wardrobe*.

Albeit the ending of chapter one suggests that the reader should have a little more faith in fortune and walk with wonder instead of distrust, the reader both naturally trusts and distrusts Mr. Tumnus. There is something about his character that causes wonder and suspicion. While the wonder is in regard to his light-hearted appearance, the suspicion is in regard to the yet unspoken motives of Mr. Tumnus. And because the default reaction of children is often seeing the bright side, Lucy does not realize Mr. Tumnus's kindness is, at least in part, deceit. Lucy is too kind and inexperienced to notice the predicament she has put herself in. Mr. Tumnus's demeanor, manners, and way with words cause the ever-trustful and starry-eyed—verging on quixotic—Lucy to be blind to the danger: all the while, the reader is, of course, thinking on Lucy's naivety and foolishness. Nevertheless, there is more to Mr. Tumnus, and the situation than first meets the eye of Lucy and the reader: both good and bad.

Maybe it is naïve to trust in fortune. Maybe it is foolish to walk with wonder. Maybe seeing the best in people and situations is short-sighted. Sometimes such a stance does lead to more trouble than one really wants to find. What eventually comes out about Mr. Tumnus does seem to suggest such ideas and confirm the reader's suspicion. Then again, whether life is trekked with trust or distrust, joy or anxiety, trouble is inevitable. Avoiding trouble is not possible and should not be the focal point of the journey called Life, but it shouldn't be forgotten that Life ought to be approached with more caution than Lucy has displayed. It is naïve to have distrust as your default. It is foolish to neglect wonderment. It is short-sighted to only see the worst in people and situations. Still, it is also a very silly thing to neglect prudence. In your day to day encounters, there is more to each person and situation than meets the eye: trust in fortune and be prudent.

In spite of our suspicion, why is it that at first sight we, along with Lucy, initially like Mr. Tumnus? In this suspicion, why do we continue to like him? When we find that he has been deceitful, why do we side with Lucy as she encourages him? Despite reasonable reservations, there is something aesthetically drawing about his appearance, which causes us to see the genuineness of his character. While it is true that there is more than meets the eye with Mr. Tumnus, Lewis has crafted Mr. Tumnus so that what meets the eye is most telling about him. Lewis has molded Mr. Tumnus so that we expect his actions to align with his appearance, to complete his character.

When the reader first sees Mr. Tumnus, he is wrapped in red and carrying what looks to be Christmas gifts in a land that has been without Christmas for (possibly) a hundred years. Moreover, the utter silliness of a pleasant-looking, reddish-skinned faun carrying an umbrella brings about a merry feeling which draws Lucy and the reader to accept him without any real fear. He looks Jovial—which means more than merry.

There are many different external and internal characteristics which, as Lewis understood them, are Jovial. In this particular instance, Lewis wants to emphasize the relationship between joy and sacrifice, merriment and heroism. This means, because Mr. Tumnus appears to be merry, we expect him to also be a help; we expect him to be the hero; we expect him to be brave. He must choose betrayal or bravery. He inevitably chooses bravery because that is Jovial: to help someone in need in spite of the danger to yourself.

Do you not often find those who have the power of laughter also have the power of boldness? Is it not a common occurrence that those who have the gift of encouragement also tend to have the courage to help others in spite of the danger to themselves? Those who light up a room with their merriment are often the ones you can call in time of need. These characteristics go hand-in-hand because they are in agreement. These characteristics are Jovial—or, at least, they are reflecting a part of Joviality.

At this juncture in *The Chronicles*, Lewis is telling us that forgiveness is a better foundation than condemnation. It may lead to a friendship that will not only save the lives and souls of those friends but cause a radiant ripple of good fortune to roll across the dimensions of time and space that will change the interactions between two different worlds in two different universes for the rest of their histories. It is in the closing of chapter two that the entire novel and its counterparts—the other six Chronicles—have their foundation. Without the mending of woes and the forgiving of guilt, Lucy and Mr. Tumnus will not be friends, and likely, Narnia will remain in winter and our world without the beauty of Narnian adventure. This is where the whole story really begins and where we begin to love this magical world, with the establishment of an unlikely friendship, rooted in the childlike forgiveness of a lion-hearted little girl.

3

Winter-Wandering and Woe

Proof?

I'm back. I'm safe.
Sorry to be so late.
It's cold there. You'll see.
The wood, the snow—it's lovely.

A game? A rouse?
No, I am not confused
Look in there. You'll know.
There's a world beyond the coats.

No wood? No snow?
An ordinary wardrobe?
I've been there! I've seen,
Even if you don't believe.

No trick. No lie.
Not a story for bedtime.
It's in there. It's true,
Even if I cannot prove.

Winter-Wandering and Woe

Woefully wandering about
Without a friend in this world,
Daring to deem truth better than
Silver and Pearl.

Boldly bearing softly,
Velvety with your valiant paws,
The daunting eyes of disbelief—
A relief to all.

Gallantly guarding your pride
Inside your loyal lion's skin—
Shining like tin in a sun-burst—
Preserves the den.

> Herald honesty high above
> The shove; sternly hold your ground.
> Ringing is the silent roar, too low,
> Below a sound.
>
> Little One, lion-hearted,
> Parted is the passing cold.
> Remember…
>
> Triumphant truth's more precious than
> Rubies and Gold.

A Meeting of Foes

Curious.
Yes, curious indeed.
My call slightly echoing,
Though the walls be not far from me.
This place, to me, is not what it seems.
Not what I was expecting.
No, not indeed.
Strange.
What a strange sound.
I hear echoing around, a sound
That does confound.
Where am I?

Wait.
Now there is the light:
The light from the room outside,
The room outside the wardrobe door.
What a curious sight; that is not the light,
Not the light I have seen before,
Shining through the open door.
What is this light?
Cold.
What is that air?
I feel it everywhere?
Frozen and crisp. Fine and bare.
Not a soul anywhere.
Where am I?

No.
Not imaginary!
Not this wood that I see.
Red is the sun, bright at its rising—
At the trunks of trees, bright and new,
Over the horizon, clear and blue.
It can't be true!
How?
How can this be?
Can my mind believe
What my eyes can see so clearly?
She will never forgive me.
Where am I?

Jingling.
Tinkling bells
Approaching fast.
The chiming of hoofs
Stamping past.
Crack!
Wisp. Snap.
Pop! Crack!
Again and again,
The air fills with the rap—
Snap. Pop! Crack!—
As the passersby
STOP!

In reply, "What am I?"

Will to be Unwavering

Have you ever experienced something so joyful as to be beyond belief? Have you ever had an experience so unique that words fail to define it? Have you ever had an experience that seemed to pull you out of this world, even if just for a moment, to see that there is life beyond your own little sphere? If so, count yourself blessed. Being able to say that you have experienced something so unique that you cannot even put it into words or that, even when you try, others simply cannot grasp it, is a wonderful thing and should be held near to your heart. Not everyone gets the chance to get a glimpse of life beyond this world, to see past the foolish fog of Western Society's need for tangible, verifiable proof. Then again, not everyone who gets a glimpse into that Other, enjoys it. In this chapter, Lewis contrasts two different kinds of people who experience the unexplainable: one which is filled with wonder and will stand by their experience no matter the cost to self (Lucy), and one which finds no joy in stumbling into an unexplainable world (Edmund).

Though it seems to be the common consensus in contemporary society that something cannot be or cannot have been unless it can be proven or repeated, the truth is most of what you believe to be true you believe without any personally verified proof, and much of what you trust to be undeniable is not falsifiable. Some things simply must be and are accepted to be true without any proof concerning how or why they are (if the world exists by chance)—like basic mathematics. Can things which are unseen and untestable not be true? Or, just because only one person has experienced something and cannot repeat it, does that make it false? Of course, the person can be a liar or delusional or insane or mistaken, but then again, maybe not. Can a person's character not stand as a possible proof to their claim?

It may be difficult, but try to put yourself in Lucy's shoes during this trying time. On top of the many other complications in her life due to the War, Lucy has just stumbled upon a whole other world where she became accustomed to things only true in fairytales. While there, she met a kind faun who kidnapped her in order to hand her over to some kind of White Witch Queen before repenting and helping her escape back home—a lot to wrap one's mind around, to say the least. And now that she has returned from her magical and terrible journey, she finds that her character is in question by those few people who are, at this moment, her whole life. She finds that the siblings she has looked up to, Susan and Peter, think she is a liar. The bond between herself and her only connection to her world is becoming more strained everyday— what a lost and helpless situation this must be. But, somehow, she handles it with grace.

It is not easy to stand against the ridicule of those who have authority over you, especially when you love them. It is hard to stand strong against the disappointment of shifting eyes, especially when you know the disappointment is filled with love for you. It is hard not to break down after days and days of pestering jabs that defame your character, especially when you know you are in the right. It is easier to give in, to either succumb to the ridicule and lie about the truth or fight back with ridicule of your own. Lucy has shown tremendous character in boldly and gently sticking to the truth. And in this, it seems that her truthfulness is not just for her own sake. Even though it means more trouble, Lucy remains gentle and lion-hearted when sticking to the truth for the sake of her Pride (her family).

Like Lucy, sometimes things happen to us that are really beyond explaining, beyond proof. And when we try to explain our wonderful experience, we only receive ridicule. We must be honest. We must stick to the truth, even if the whole world considers us crazy. Courageously standing up for what we know to be true matters more than the uninformed jabs of others.

Unlike Lucy, Edmund is not so cheerful when he stumbles into the frozen world behind the coats, and neither is the party that cuts off his wandering. As he feels around in the dark, Edmund's uncertainty is not accompanied with an air of joy or wonder. Once the dense boy finally figures where he is, his snobbish, whiny, melancholy, and wearisome character is exacerbated. Confusion and apprehension are what define this moment with

Edmund, not calm curiosity. He represents a character which is in stark opposition to Joviality.

Lewis uses the cold, startling rush of reindeer, a dwarf, and a great white (unfriendly) lady to put lead in the shoes of any mirth left in the reader. In Edmund's unpleasant attitude and snarky distaste for this Other world, Lewis prepares the reader for a very different kind of meeting between Edmund and the White Witch than the one between Lucy and Mr. Tumnus. Trouble is afoot.

Is it a coincidence that those who carry around a troubled heart in their chest find trouble wherever they go? Not that this meeting would turn out good for even the most lighthearted person or that a mere perspective change could have really prevented any bad from coming out of this meeting, but as Edmund treks through the forest, the reader can tell by his attitude that even if he were to run into Father Christmas, he would have made the worst of it. Good character, a good attitude, and a hopeful perspective will not prevent bad from happening in this world or any other; nevertheless, it can encourage a person to look past the surrounding darkness and find that beam of light which reveals that, in the end, trouble will not have the last word.

4

A Disastrous Delight

An Unpleasant Conversation

Speak what I want to hear
Or you will find that I can't hear.
Tickle my ears or you will meet my spear.
    Should I know what to speak?
    How should I know you are a queen?
    All I know is I am cold and hungry.

Tell me now what you are.
You must have traveled very far
Not to know that I am Queen in these parts.
    A boy on holiday,
    Not a dwarf—I have never shaved—
    The younger boy of four, by the way.

Two plus two, did you say?
But, are the others on their way?
What a great surprise that would be today!
    You want to meet those three?
    (Nothing special compared to me.)
    Yes, two sons and daughters of Adam and Eve.

Bow to my will, stupid boy.
You will regret being so coy.
Don't annoy! Don't annoy or you I'll destroy.
    Pity my foolish tongue;
    Please understand that I am young
    And haven't begun to learn how words are spun.

Ah, yes. Now, let me think.
Well, how about a nice warm drink?
But, what good is a drink without a treat?
> *Give me what I want to taste*
> *Or you will find that I can't taste.*
> *Please my palette or I'll be gone with haste.*

My dearest, take a bite
You will find it is a delight—
Enchanted, you'll want to eat every bite.
> *Please. O' please, one more treat?*
> *For a taste, I'll do anything.*
> *Yes. I will return with the other three.*

A Disastrous Delight

Yes, pour the poor and retched soul a drink.
Drink up and pore over your souls delight.
Served, you can be with me and rule. Just think;
Servants galore and treats filled to the brink.

Above the sifted snow, let go one drop.
Magically sweet, a slope, easy to slip:
One pound, two pounds, one more, one more—can't stop!
Sticky fingers now clasp the case—EMPTY.
Messy, a sulking face with powdered plea

A trick, not treat: deceit touches the lips.
A weakness comes with cold, down deep inside.
Soft and foamy, a drink of vain hubris.
With pain, winter does grow and joy subsides—
In isolated hush, envy delights.

Opposite Opinions

Ooh! How fun! How fun!
I'm happy to see
It's not just me.
What fun this will be.

Ooh! Hoorah . . . hoorah!
We can celebrate,
You've found your way.
What games we will play.

Ooh! Come on. Come on.
We've so much to tell.
They're in this as well.
It feels like a spell.

> *UGH! I KNOW. I KNOW.*
> *I'm tired of the snow.*
> *I'm shivering with cold.*
> *I want to go home.*

The Conversation can be Changed

The most unpleasant kind of conversation that can be taken up is the kind between those who converse only to achieve their own ends. Such conversations are not a source of real delight and often lead to disaster. They weigh heavily on the soul. I think it would be appropriate to call such conversations Saturnine: so unheard they might as well not be spoken; so rotten their jar is better left unopen; so cold, uncouth, and self-serving they leave their participants drained; so foul and distasteful they are nothing more than conversation feigned. It is this type of conversation that Lewis uses to open up chapter four and introduce us to the Witch and her schemes in-person, as well as uncover Edmund's gravest flaws.

As with Tumnus and Lucy, the Witch and Edmund meet under the spiritual influence of a certain planet (theirs is Saturn). However, while the fortunate planet (Jupiter) truly rules over Tumnus and Lucy, and therefore any negative element in their character is canceled out by the other, the Witch and Edmund's servitude to the unfortunate planet (Saturn) cancels out any positive elements (if there are any) and they are only left with the negative elements of their respective characters.

Also, like Tumnus and Lucy, these two meet at cross purposes. Yet, where Tumnus' and Lucy's cross purposes are redirected to align under Joviality, the Witch and Edmund are driven further apart with every passing moment under the reigns of Saturninity.

Lewis charmingly pens this scene so that it perfectly contrasts with the Jovial meeting of Tumnus and Lucy. The entire chapter is only enjoyable in the sense that it is well-written and is thoughtfully placed in the story's arc. Other than that, the chapter alarms us, disgusts us, and even angers us at the cruel cunning of the Witch and the foolish envy of Edmund. Lewis has placed this meeting in just the right place to highlight that neither Edmund nor the Witch are Jovial characters: they do not seek or see good fortune wherever they go. This meeting and conversation reveal these two as seekers, finders, and creators of misfortune wherever they go—the Witch with full intention and Edmund, mostly, by mere childish ignorance.

As the chapter comes to a close, we begin to actually see the character contrast between Edmund and Lucy. When Lucy, the ever-excitable, sees Edmund, she is overcome with the possibilities of shared adventures. As a kid especially, it is no fun to go on adventures all alone. It is best to share your adventures with those you love. Also, Lucy sees that her holding on to truth has not been for nothing. She has a great reason to celebrate, but the dark forces of Saturn will not give in so easily. Edmund, on the other hand, does not share Lucy's festive attitude. True to his character, he remains secretive and unpleasant. Even in the conversation with Lucy, Edmund refocuses the pleasantries to talk of his own cold misfortune.

Does chapter four remind you of some of your own leanings to self-centeredness when conversing with friends? Does this chapter remind you of your own weaknesses and jealousies, your own inability to let down your scepter of control, and the dreary parts of your own character that at times displays itself in how you choose to steer conversations? Sometimes we go into conversations only to get what we want or to be told what we want to hear: sometimes we initiate a talk in order to get something from the other party: sometimes we start up conversations for the sake of justifying our foul longings. Too often we are, in a sense, conversation partners who are no different from the Witch and Edmund. But we can, if we open our eyes to our own weaknesses, use our mouth's rudder to be better conversation companions.

Although *The Lion, the Witch and the Wardrobe* would be a rather lackluster tale and untrue to humanity if an element of err was lacking, Edmund's downfall and the Witch's opposition to wholesomeness find their real beauty and meaning for us as humans in their defeat. What makes our life excitable and beautiful, what separates humanity from the beasts, is not err, but the conquering of it. The story of our life is filled with weakness and envy. It is hindered by cold, calculated ambition. But, it is also able to be amended with gracious mercy. We can steer our conversations from self-focus to shared-focus. We can turn from the separating powers of Saturn to the conjoining powers of Jupiter. And most of all, the final word in the conversation between ourselves and God on this earth—that thing we call Life—can be grace.

5

Of Others' Worlds

A Baneful Blow

Sometimes, when the bond of blood runs cold,
Even Leonines cease to be bold;
Even heroes, for a time, will fold;
Even breaks, the chief cornerstone.

There is a draught, hardest of all to swallow:
A cup that causes laughter to run hollow;
A sickly draft which death so often follows;
A pestilence, few apply the antidote.

Betrayer of blood. Traitor of country.
A baneful blow within a family.
What can remedy this sad villainy?
Humility, forgiveness, love, and mercy.

Logic and Other Worlds

Look up. Think with the stars, wandering hearts.
With eyes you see, and think you know the truth.
Somewhere beyond your heart, beyond the stars,
There's more to truth than can be seen or proved:

Shadows in caves; silhouettes on the wall;
Echoes . . . echoes . . . roll in . . . grottos . . . grottos.
Away! The chains. Away. Your world's so small.
Surely you know, you must, if you've read Plato.

The choice is yours to map the odds and ends:
Where music's waves and harmony's ridge merge.
The scale, the line you hold in your own hands.
Measure. Find where common and sacred verge.

But, remember this rule and please permit:
Not your affair? Keep your nose out of it.

On the Shore of Joy's Bay

Sing with the folding of Fortune!
Sing with the spinning of Fate
On the shore of Joy's bay.

Fate or Fortune? Fortune or Fate?
There's only one tune at heights so great—
Far past the dark side of the Moon.

Free-will? Destiny? What do they mean
On the plane where Mirth and men meet,
In the valley where Victory gives birth?

Fate or Fortune? Choice or Chosen?
In the glade where pardon is spoken—
Where Fortune, Fate, and Free-will fade—

Sing with the toiling of Fortune!
Sing with the chosen of fate
On the shore of Joy's bay.

Of Others' Worlds

Pride is among the most fatal of weapons in the arsenal of human emotions. In many of the great tragedies in history—both fictional and non-fictional—pride has led to the spilling of much innocent blood. When thinking on the real danger of pride, we must not forget Macbeth's bloodlust or Hitler's megalomaniacal march across Europe; however, pride's perilous impact is not limited to such scales. The most significant actions of pride are committed in the day to day, between one person and another. The most fretful and ubiquitous pride is that which daily drives families and friends to split with little hope of re-bonding. As shown in chapter five, such daily misuse of pride holds back the helping hand, blinds the eyes to others' worlds, and pries into the business of others. Yet, pride's lethal and regrettable capabilities are, like any weapon, only truly dangerous to the innocent when wielded in the wrong hands.

As chapter five opens, one of the saddest parts of the book commences: Edmund breaks his little sister's heart. Although Edmund has just finished making a deal with the evil one, he has a chance to put that behind him. He has a chance to reach out a helping hand to someone who should be under his protection. He has a chance to go against his treacherous promise and chivalrously stand with his little-sister. He has a chance to use his pride against evil. Instead, he chooses to slap the needful hand with a force that rifts more than just the soul of the one he has betrayed. This choice causes a rippling rift to split the already weak bonds between himself and all his siblings. This willful act of pride will eventually lead to the death of many.

Following Edmund's claim that he has never been in Narnia and was only leading Lucy on, even Peter and Susan begin to suspect the worst of Lucy. They are so blind to the possibility that this other world of Lucy's may actually exist, that there could even be worlds other than their own, that they begin to think Lucy is insane. It may not seem that such a thought is based out of pride, but it is. They are convinced that if they cannot get there, if they cannot see it for themselves, it cannot be there. In their pride, Peter and

Susan cannot see the twining of fate, the wheel of fortune, nor the will of Jove. They cannot see the truth in the eyes of an innocent girl nor the lies in the eyes of a devious boy.

In a state that they believe to be logical-concern, Peter and Susan go to the Professor for help with their mentally ailing sister. Of course, we can all sympathize with the older siblings. Would we not think our little sister was off her rocker? Would we not want to try to get her help as soon as possible? But the help the Professor gives is quite different than any could expect. The Professor is a man of different pride, Platonism-pride. He is a man that trusts logic's foundation is not in the shadows we think are reality. He believes the possibility of others' worlds are, if weighed properly, quite logical.

With this logical practice on full display, the Professor reveals to Peter and Susan that their concerns are the illogical practice of an inept school system. The Professor helps them understand the strangeness of the situation: they trust what they know to be true—there is no such thing as other worlds—while also denying something else they know to be true—their sister is not a liar. With sharp wit, the Professor cuts their pride to the quick by suggesting their concern is merely an overreaction of busybodies.

Quite typical for a great literary artist like Lewis, this chapter comes to a close with a beautiful cliffhanger. A cliffhanger that leaves the observant reader on the edge of more than one seat: not only may the reader be left wondering whether or not the children are about to stumble into Narnia, the reader may also be left pondering the question of fate versus free will—a question that seems, on the surface, to be unrelated to pride. It seems to me that the more one tries to wrap their head around whether or not the Pevensies are fated to go into Narnia, go into Narnia by their own free will, or end up in Narnia due to some kind of mixture of fate and free will, the more one begins to realize that there is a place where fate, fortune, and free will fade. And in that place, so does pride.

Truly, it is the prideful man that tries to prove that no one, not even God, controls his fortune; and yet, is the one who spends their time trying to figure out if they are one of God's chosen favorite not stuck in a similar pride? Whether a man chooses to go into the wardrobe and chooses to fight evil, or the Emperor has destined them to conquer long ago, does not really matter in the heat of battle. When one is able to, or forced to, relieve themselves of self-concern, to be humbled enough that their pride can be pure, such ideas cease to matter. There is a place where the spinning of the Fates ceases to matter, where Fortune's wheel has no say: in the moment; where God is. For, ironically enough, it is in the moment that we can touch eternity.

And in the moment of this chapter's closing, the Pevensies seem to be forced by unforeseen circumstances to go into the Wardrobe, the door to another world. In this moment, they do not question, they do not think, they simply run like startled children. At this moment, they do the most logical thing a group of young children do when they know they might find themselves face to face with an adult that may scold them, they hide. In this moment, without realizing it, they step further into a greater plan where they will be forced to make the toughest decisions of their lives thus far. They are stepping into a world where the type of pride that defines their head and heart will take form as a weapon for good or evil.

6

Certainly Surprised

Certainly Surprised

What's this?
This tingling in the air . . .
    By Jove!
    It's wet everywhere.

What's this?
This chill in my nose . . .
    By Jove!
    Trees covered with snow.

What's this?
This winter surprise . . .
    By Jove!
    A twinkling daylight.

What's this?
This rift between worlds . . .
    By Jove!
    New worlds to explore.

What's this?
This certain truth-slip . . .
    By Jove!
    Regret filled silence.

What's this?
This need to repent . . .
    By Jove!
    No need to pretend.

Where Honor Lies

From left to right, a trying line
Pawed deep into the frozen crust.
Cross this line and you will find
A test of trust from dawn till dusk.

From right to left, a telling view
Cut right across these tearing eyes.
Into view, what you will choose
With friendly eyes, where honor lies.

From rise till fall and under stars,
From step to step, no going back.
Trust the stars and cross that bar.
Don't draw back once you've stepped past.

Following the Flycatcher

I cannot catch it; but I will follow it,
This catcher that catches me.
I do not dare, though I don't know where
This catcher that catches me
Will lead me from here, ask whence or where—
You catcher that catches me.
Is he friend or foe? Can I surely know
This catcher that catches me?
Still I move in with a faith in
This catcher that catches me.
Speak to me now, someway, somehow—
O catcher that catches me.
With wondrous words no ear has heard,
You catcher that catches me,
Open my eyes to see your plans for me,
You catcher that catches me.
And when I arrive I will realize
My catcher has caught me.

Faithfully Following the Bird

It is surprising how certain we can be about things, and still be certainly wrong. How one chooses to handle a world-shaking surprise that turns their certainty on its head will reveal the source of that certainty. If the source is faith in one greater than themselves, they will accept it in good faith, no matter how difficult. If the source is pride in their own superior knowledge, they will reject it to the ruin of their souls. Like the Apostle Paul's encounter with Christ on the Road to Damascus, Peter and Susan are about to be confronted by a truth that will knock them off their proverbial donkey. Their certainty is about to be turned upside down. And as Paul's character of passion for truth was fully uncovered and converted once that reality-reshaping beam of Jesus as Messiah struck his eyes, so will the honorable characters of Peter and Susan be tried and found true once that thrust of red dawn shines through the Narnian wood.

Further and further into the wardrobe they move. Moment after moment, something strange begins to unearth itself. This is not an ordinary wardrobe. They are no longer in the only world they have known to exist and have found themselves standing in the middle of a foreign wood. For Peter and Susan, this does not lead to a distasteful reaction like Edmund, but a reaction of wonder—mixed with a little fear—more akin to Lucy. Without question, Peter and Susan feel a need to apologize for disbelief in this new world and Lucy's character. An apology which is followed by mending of more than the slightly torn relationship between themselves and Lucy; they reconnect their hearts to that childish trust in Jovian wonder and adventure that was expressed in the book's opening, a trust that will lead to a disheartening discovery and testing predicament.

In this redeemed air, the party decides it best to follow Lucy in their newfound adventure land; but this adventure quickly turns into a graver endeavor than they could have imagined. With every step in this new world, they find themselves further from the secured certainty on the other side of the wardrobe doors. At the sight of Tumnus's torn cave and the letter of arrest, they find that they are not only in tangible foreign terrain, they are now dealing with decisions of the heart that will deliver nothing but new spiritual struggle upon new spiritual struggle. Though there is no honor among thieves, there is honor between friends. They (at least Peter and Susan) choose to honor this friend of Lucy. An honorable choice which will be followed by an act of faith that Edmund will see as a foolish stumbling block.

While trying to figure out how they might aid Tumnus, the reddest breasted robin (Old World Flycatcher) appears. Lacking options, they take a leap of faith and decide to follow this peculiar guide, for it seems to know more than it can say. While they cannot be certain of the bird's intentions, they follow its lead. They trust the bird will lead them through the unknown. Because the red-breasted bird appears jovial, they are certain it must be friendly—in Lewis's world, this is the case.

This act of faith can truly be likened to the life of the Christian as we follow that Holy Bird (dove) who silently leads us through unknown terrain to a destination that we cannot find without Him. This act of faith is also meant to lead the reader to follow the spirit which Lewis has set to be followed. Yet, it is in this uncertainty that Edmund speaks against the act of faith, against the bird. Under the guise of apprehension, Edmund tries to figure out how to take all eyes off the bird and lead them away from the quest of valor. Of course, Edmund's statement against this act does seem to have logic to it; however, like Judas Iscariot, his logic is not based on faith or honest concern. Edmund's reasons are based on selfish motives.

In this ever-growing test, the spirit which rules over each of the siblings strengthens. In this spiritual strengthening, the split between those who seek honorable ends, and are willing to step into uncertain situations with seemingly blind certainty (those under Jove), and the one who desires to flee trouble for self, or only go further for selfish ends with certainty in his own superiority (the one under Saturn), stretches to the brink.

There comes a time in our own lives when we must also decide to follow the bird into uncertainty, and find that we are certainly wrong, or turn back in err. Lewis leads us to follow the bird with the childlike faith of at least three of the Pevensies. May we also choose to walk with such faith when such uncertain situations arise.

7

A Helping Hand

TRUSTS

And suddenly it seems that I walk unguided
Into terrain unknown to me.
Once the flutter in my heart's subsided,
I will take in my surroundings.

Caution:
T—read lightly.
    R—uffled with every step.

Danger:
U—nknown shadows.
    S—wiftly, a passing glimpse.

Faith:
T—ough choices.
    S—till, I take the risk

And suddenly I feel their guidance, though unseen.
Ever those hands, they are guiding,
Guiding blind men like me.

He Moves

Over the sands, from untraversed lands,
Over the sea comes unchartedly
The Powerful One—the Emperor's Son.
His gifts in tow, He moves. He moves . . .
Across vast woods, in between worlds,
Across galaxies, fulfills prophecies
With a gentle roar heard from afar.
With aid in droves, He moves. He moves . . .
Through the Cosmos, the Almighty Host,
Turning with speed no other exceeds.
With Conquering care, the Great Comforter,
Our help and hope, He moves. He moves . . .

A Helping Hand

A hushing hand resting against lips
Whose teeth protrude with significance.
A whiskered snout whispering secrets.
This proud stout fisherman's insignificant
Size begs the question of his prominence.

Why, Good Fortune, has this help been sent?
What good can come from such help as this?

Wisdom, honor, and nerve are indeed
The qualities that Good Fortune deems
Fit for the help that Jove's children need.
So the wheel stops here with humbled beasts
Whose worth is so much more than it seems.

A dainty hand, nimbly sewing thread,
Whose care worn paws work for other's ends.
A loving heart that bakes comfort's bread.
This meek seamstress's kindly crowned head
Will dam up doubt and put it to bed.

This is why Good Fortune has sent you
These modest beasts—the warm, ruddered two.

Choosing a Path

Good fortune may, as men see it, fall on anyone at any time; but, there is a prerequisite to looking along good fortune—trust. Trust in the midst of the unknown is required to see any fortune as good because one can never really know whether or not their fortune is truly good until its benefits are reaped. Then again, the one who trusts in the Emperor and his son will ultimately find that all fortune is good, while the one without trust in that great Emperor can, in the end, only grieve in pure chance that is neither good nor bad. Granted, those who have lived in Narnia for the past century do not feel as if good fortune has been a part of their lives, and the Pevensies likely find their current situation disagreeable, the maker of fortune will cause all fortunes to unite for good's triumph in the end. In the trials ahead, the Pevensies and the good beasts of Narnia must learn to trust in the Fortune Maker. In this trust, their vision will be cleared so that they may look along fortune and see its goodness.

Chapter seven opens with another predicament that will take the second of many leaps of faith. The children find that their winged guide has jetted from sight. While still in shock, a disquieting rustle begins to dodge around them. It turns out to be a talking beaver who claims to be friendly. This claim is met with an understandable reservation. Still, aided by a supposed token of assurance, Lucy's handkerchief, they accept the helping hands that have been provided. The children follow the beaver to his home where they help prepare dinner. Here they are going to receive an account of the troubles they have landed themselves in. Moreover, at this strange dinner table the children are to hear news of the fortune which has befallen them and learn of some kind of king who has begun his move against the Witch in order to bring better fortunes back to Narnia.

Maybe these young few have not yet come to the point in their life-walk where they grasp the importance of faith; nevertheless, their parents must have instilled a trusting spirit in them. They do not know if the fortune that has come their way is good or not. They have not yet heard the tale or prophecies that have caused others to risk their necks to save them. They do not know if the bird or beaver are actually friends or foes, though chances are quite good by the end of chapter seven. They do not know if this king they have heard mention of is good or evil. But an urge of trust seems to guide them, and they take the risk.

Blind chance does not exist for those who trust in God. But blind trust definitely does. Such blindness does, at times, have its setbacks; yet, for the faithful, Fortune makes a way. By the time all the Pevensies really question the bird's loyalties, they are already hip-deep in prophecy. By the time they wonder about the return journey, they are already past the point of no return. Even though the Pevensies are given a token of good faith on which their trust can have a certain amount of assurance, that this token was actually given in good faith or that following the one who has it is the best idea is an act of faith that could end in a bad way. It does not. The controller of fortune (Fortuna Major) honors their act of faith, which is becoming a more readily used part of at least three of the four children's repertoire.

These four have, albeit not on purpose, stepped into a story written long before they were born in their own world and long before they tread snow in Narnia. Without realizing it, they have been guided by more than a robin. They have been guided by powers unknown, beyond their limited vision, and below the surface of their consciousness. While they surely chose to blindly follow the bird and choose to follow and have dinner with the beavers (What other choice do they have?), the choice has not completely come of their own accord. The writer of their story (and I don't mean Lewis) destined these choices to be placed in front of them, and they have freely chosen, in faith, to take the risk.

In the end, we must all decide to take one risk or another. Will we risk the foolishness of faith? Or, will we choose to hold on to that short cord we call physical reality that is resting against the sharp scissors of the Fates? Hopefully, before the end comes, our eyes will have adjusted to look along Fortune and see Goodness itself shining beyond and through the mountains and valleys ahead that we must tread. At any moment, the cord will be snipped, and then all faith will be counted for. Those who have only trusted in the physical cord they can touch, those who have measured fortune with their own span, will be cut off. Those who have trusted in the Cord Maker will find a brand new cord, never to be cut. Those whose only light came through the physical eye will be consumed by the shadows: they will be blind. Those whose light came from that burning fire beyond the forms will finally behold, eternally, the Form Maker.

8

Not Safe, but Safety

In Courts of Stone

Tick . . . Tick . . . Tick . . . Tick . . .
The secondhand ticks.
The snowflake hits
The icy ground,
Piles all around.
Tick . . . Tick . . . Tick . . . Tick . . .
Minute by minute,
Row upon row,
Times passes by
These courts of stone—
Tick . . . Tick . . . Tick . . . Tick . . .
—laden with frost,
Echo what's lost.
Souls lost to time's
Ritual rhyme:
Tick . . . Tick . . . Tick . . . Tick . . .
Hours, then days,
Seasons, and months;
Forever alone
In courts of stone.
Tick . . . Tick . . . Tick . . . Tick . . .
Can they be saved?
Is there a way
To rectify
These slaves of time's
Tick . . . Tick . . . Tick . . . Tick . . .

Not Safe, but Safety

Hardened is the way, and far from safety,
To peace and victory, goodness and bravery.
This is His way: certainly Good, not safe.

Only the gallant few, who have courage to choose,
Will trod the path of peace, never with ease.
This is His amity: it's Good, but not easy.

Fearful is the journey, and fear the key
That opens virtue's gate, and inside something waits—
It is His shelter: Good and forever.

So tremble with wonder, and rejoice with terror,
For broad is sorrow, His passage, narrow.
He is the Good, and certainly misunderstood.

To Forgive or Not to Forgive

There is a knife that cuts to the marrow,
A blade that splits apart the ligaments,
Whose sheath is bound with treacherous sorrow,
Whose piercing thrust divides closest of kin.

There is a flame that burns without control,
A blaze so hot many dare not contain,
Whose heat and ash and smoke can choke the soul,
Whose furnace bends and shapes envy's weapon.

There is a spark that sets men's heart aflame,
A strike that lights with petulant design,
Whose ignition will find a life to claim,
Whose catalyst is avarice and pride.

Nevertheless, a party must be sent
To liberate the man from his lament.

> But this party must be greater than men:
> Only One can turn back the ignition.

Walking the Path

We all walk down our own path: a path where time and fortune converge: a path pieced together by choices and consequences, though not all the consequences we face are due to our own choices. Sometimes this path is full of friends. Sometimes this path is lonely. Sometimes we are lost in the woods. Sometimes we know exactly where we are going. Sometimes we take the right path, sometimes the wrong. Whether alone or accompanied, whether lost or on familiar ground, right or wrong, we all walk our own path.

Since before the book began, tensions have been growing, and will come to a breaking point, between Edmund and the other three siblings, especially Peter. Due to various clashes and rivalries that are typical between siblings, many routes have been carved through the dense wood of troubles these children have been tossed into. Each of the children have cut their way through their circumstances with differing choices that have, at points, led them completely out of one another's sight. However, Lucy's, Susan's, and Peter's have, as they sit at the dinner table in Mr. and Mrs. Beaver's house, begun to intertwine and create a single lane. Edmund's course, on the other hand, has been steadily carved through the densest forest in a direction that continually puts a greater distance between himself and his siblings. By the time the fish have finished frying, there is no longer a hope that his way will intersect with his siblings without the aid of another, greater path maker.

Essentially, two roads have begun to be traveled by the children. One, traveled by the three, will lead to the Leonine leader. The other, traveled by that lonely soul (Edmund), will lead to the stony court where time ticks as an eternal enemy—that icy castle where death might actually be a relief. The three's Leonine path will prove to be difficult; but it will also be filled with friendship, a hope of fulfilling prophecies, and the beautiful thought that, when the road is ended, they will see Aslan face to face. Edmund's path will prove to be even more difficult because his only company will be jealousy, disappointment, misery, anger, and uncertainty.

The further into dinner, conversation, and prophecy the company gets, the thicker the wood grows that is cutting off Edmund from the rest. Edmund's loathsome feelings at the name of Aslan give a hint to the growing distance between himself and the right road. As the excitement comes to a head, Edmund is able to finally sneak off without notice. How could he get up from the table without being seen? How could he walk right out the door without notice? He cannot be that sneaky. I think this definitely speaks to Edmund's unimportance to the party and might give us a little reason to sympathize with this lost and lonely soul.

While speaking with the Beavers, the three realize they are being called to take on an adventure they were surely not looking for—a path that must be tread for honor's sake, an adventure that must be taken in order to save Tumnus and all of Narnia. According to prophecy, they must set off to meet and join the Lion and conquer Winter. They must move forward on an unsafe journey, to bow to an unsafe leader, and meddle in business that is, I am sure in their minds, none of their own. The weight of their situation builds with every ancient rhyme that whistles through Mr. Beaver's teeth. And, before the chapter is over, they will see that they must take this adventure in faith if they want to save their treasonous brother. They must decide to go on, even in fear, and meet with that good, unsafe king if they are going to somehow bring their brother back from his forsaken road. Once they realize that Edmund has fled from dinner and, thanks to Mr. Beaver's frankness, gone to betray them all to the Queen, the three begin to understand their business in this world. They must continue on their course.

Just like we see in the story of Lucy, Edmund, Susan, and Peter, every choice you make, even the smallest, seemingly insignificant choice leads you further down a path that you could never travel had you made a different choice just a millisecond ago. Right now, inside your body, neurons and axons are at work, initiating muscle movements to fulfill the commands coming from your brain. Right now, while reading these words, thoughts of unconnected things are flying in and out of your head (chores, itches, random daydreams, that embarrassing moment in middle school when you accidentally . . .). Right now, your body is performing thousands of instinctual functions that you are not even aware of. With each passing second, these sent commands, fleeting thoughts, unseen activities, and other various actions and decisions are sending you (and those around you) down a path that will one day reach its cut off.

Every minute, even those minutes which pass by without conscious thought, you travel a little further down a road that can never be retraced—time will not allow it. Probably more often than not, you misstep on this road and wish you could step back, but you really cannot. Your choice has been made, and your step has been taken. You are condemned to be free, to choose and travel the path you will, save for the path that travels back in time—it is not there. You are a slave to time's tick: you cannot go back: time will push your fate on, even if you are still as stone. Nevertheless, there is a choice that can be made on this fateful journey, here and now, that will redeem every misstep and abolish Father Time's lordship, a choice that will soon be exemplified in the life of all the Pevensie siblings, seeking forgiveness from Father Time's Lord. In his forgiveness, the constraints of time are stripped away. He transcends time, and so does his redemption.

9

COLD, COLD, COLD

Cold Travel: If I Were King

If I were king,
Woods would be razed
And roads be paved for My feet.
    Then again, if I were king,
    I would not walk—I'd be carried.

If I were king,
There would be treats
Piled to the sky, just for Me.
    Because, if I were king,
    All would be done for Me.

If I were king,
They would pay
For all they've said to Me.
    Then again, when I am king,
    Forgiveness they will beg from Me.

If I were king,
They would bow,
With faces down to My feet.
    Because, when I am king,
    No one will refuse Me.

Cold Courtyard

Like knights and rooks, bishops and pawns, each takes its square;
   No power to move on, until their player moves.
      Who are the two who play this cold, weary chess-game?
Like specters of an age long past, with fixed blank stare,
   They stand or lay unmoved, waiting to be set loose.
      With snow built up like dust, like years-untouched chess-game.

I see the pawns; but where's the King . . . the King of beasts?
   Aha! He's there. Fixed too . . . No need to fear this fool.
      The Queen has done Him in; this game is all the same.
         No King of beasts; in fact, He is the least of beasts.
            No fun left in this game.

Cold Queen

Empty-handed you've come before the Queen.
You fool! You dare stand there within my sight
Without a thing to show; no prize for me?
Look here! While laughing I will take your life.
A traitor comes and thinks he'll find delight.
A liar speaks and thinks he'll find a place
To sit and rule with my scepter beside.
Forget your news; it's time to move with haste
On sledge, through snow, we'll go with haunting pace.

A Cold Crossroad of Err

It seems to be a common consensus among mankind that the further you go down the wrong path, the harder it is to turn back. Actually, I think it might be truer to say that the longer you know you are on the wrong path, the harder it is to turn back. I believe the main cause of reluctance in such a situation is pride. It is one thing to go down the wrong path unknowingly; it is quite another thing to flick the metaphorical white-gowned angel off your shoulder telling you to turn back—"Stop! This is the wrong way. This way will only hurt you."—or to push against the thorny briar of conscience, ever-jabbing and further inflicting your soul. It is this acknowledged path of error that is the coldest and loneliest road of all; every inch gained is colder, lonelier, angrier, and more destructive than the inch before; with each passing moment, hard-conquered obstructions block the weary traveler's return—pride will not allow these victories to be overturned by conscience. With pun most definitely intended, Edmund surely knows he has chosen the cold and lonely road of err; and the further he goes, the closer he gets to his greatest sin.

After stepping out into the snowy night, Edmund's fortune begins to falter with every footprint left in the white sift. Freezing, without a jacket, banging his knee on stones hidden by the night, fighting his way through an unfamiliar wood to an icy castle where a pretentious Queen (who nearly murdered him not many days before) waits with a devilish treat, Edmund's bitterness turns to petulant hate. Other than the promise of Turkish Delight, the only warm hope in his darkening heart is the supposed inheritance that awaits him in the Witch's castle: to rule in a foreign country of eternal winter. Not much of a prize if you ask me, but this boy's mind cannot see past the blizzard of stone-cold hatred and promise of power over his siblings. So he pushes on, through fear, reluctance, and weariness, to the Witch's empty promises.

Edmund's first step into the Witch's courtyard is one of jolting shock. He sees what he believes to be Aslan himself. After waiting for an incalculable time, he realizes that this shocking lion-figure is nothing more than a statue of its former self, covered with dust-like snow as if the maid of the castle had neglected to clean this statue for months. This is where he shows his true nature, both bad and good. Like so many immature boys have done, Edmund decides to practice the art of graffiti in order to show some form of authority. Yet, once he has finished marking on the supposed Aslan statue, the magnificence of the beast causes Edmund to find no satisfaction in the thing he has done. Underneath this peevish boy's frosted skin, there is a recognition of wrong. There is no fun for him in this court of stone. Still, as many of us would do, he indignantly continues in err to more shocking revelations.

As soon as Edmund is pretty certain all the dangerous beings around him are harmless figurines, he attempts to step over a large wolf—not a good idea. Maugrim's open mouth dashes Edmund's false courage against that chilled rock in his chest. After a frightening conversation with the wolf, Edmund is called to come before the Witch. It is here that the greatest shock comes to Edmund, the Witch is furious with him—Edmund has not upheld his end of the bargain.

Standing in the presence of the Witch's Saturnine fury, Edmund quickly comes to the realization that his deal was always hopeless and one-sided. He did not keep his end of the deal because he was not clever enough. The Witch never intended to keep her end of the deal. In the end, evil will not share the crown. Just as Saturn ate his children, so the Witch plans to devour these children at any cost. If the Witch got her way, all who could possibly oppose her, including Edmund, would meet a grim demise. She is cold in every sense of the word.

Often the wrong path is taken to reach a false goal set by a devious force. Without realizing it, Edmund has struck a deal with the devil in an almost Faustian fashion. Different only in that he did not go seeking the devil, like St. Theophilus or Faustus or Robert Johnson, Edmund has sold his soul at a crossroad for nothing more than selfish desire. But now the price must be paid: Edmund must commit treason or die. In this kind of deal, the devil always wins, for the devil is clever enough to make a deal that will likely end in his favor. But if it does not, he is the devil; is he known for faithful honesty?

10

A New Day Dawning

Preparing for Pursuit

The pursuit is afoot; we must be on our way.
Queen or her cronies, it doesn't matter which
Comes with a fury. We can't afford to stay
To pack away too long, would be a mistake.
Steal away, we must, and flee from the Witch
To a hiding place: a secret for such days.
Kill is what they'll do, if we're caught in pursuit,
And gladly lick our bones; but still we can't forget
To take what we need and put treasures away.
Destroy the thought, and leave the old sowing machine.

Pad-Pad-Pad

Pad-pad-pad—Panting on.
Onward-onward. March-march.
Pad-pad-pad—Pushing-on.
Upward-upward. Climb-climb.
Swish-swish-swish—Trekking-forth.
Forward-forward. Go-go.
Swish-swish-swish—Trudging-through.
Frontward-frontward. Move-move . . .

    And when you pant,
    Push right on
    To the rest that waits.

    And when you trek,
    Trudge right through
    To the gifts of fate.

A New Day Dawning

Once a new day was dawning for five on the run
When their captain heard something that was curious:
'Twas the sound of bells jingling away 'cross their path;
So he scurried to see as the sound's author passed,
Where the jingling was heading, then something at last
Put the captain in spirits of wonder and dance.

There the four held their breath and, in fear for their lives,
Kept their ears peeled to hear the good captain's faint cry
Of good news or 'run quick'; but to their great surprise,
The good captain's voice rang with the bliss of delight.

Then their four breaths exhaled as they scurried themselves
To the top of the cave where the captain did wait.
And there stirring, good captain did stir with a clap
Of loud glee, the good captain's cold four saw the rap:

On a sledge, mounted high, a long-waited big man—
With white hair and red sash, and with gifts in his hand—
Gave a laugh, a big laugh, to assure his new friends
That his reigns and reindeer had now come through at last.

As he spoke he gave hope, and the five felt alive
In his words for they heard Father Christmas's list
Of their gifts for hard-times—a new hope. A new stride
To bring life, a new dawn full of mirth and so crisp.
Now the five stood steady as this Saint, Nicholas,
Gave them treats, warm and sweet; then dismissed like a wisp.

While he rode fast away "Merry Christmas" he praised,
For the King had arrived, and was calling his pride
By the voice of this Saint—the jolly and yet grave—
Nick.

A Joyful Journey

Despair acts like a lead weight in your shoes: it makes it awfully hard to move. Conversely, fear is a great motivator: with feverish jolts that raise your hair on edge, it energizes every movement. Still, joy is greater than these: an inside joke, a loving jest, or an acknowledged silly worry can supply a needed peace, whether in despair or fear. When standing in a dark room, it is the light shining through the crack in the door that overtakes the surrounding despair and fear: it is the light that symbolizes the waiting levity. In our hearts, we know that darkness hides all the good that truly surrounds us: that is why we fear it. Once the sun shines in its zenith, no shadow will be left: everything will be seen as it truly is. There will be no need for despair or fear. Each moment of gaiety is a crack of light coming through the door that melts winter's reign, which leads to eternal noon.

Although the three remaining siblings are definitely in a state of despair as chapter ten opens, once they understand that they will not be able to get Edmund back without the help of this lion they have heard tell about, fear of the wrath that will arrive soon overtakes them. Nevertheless, this chapter is not strictly governed by despair or fear. Because this chapter is about the flight of Jove's children, Lewis has made sure to give even the more serious moments an air of levity. Not to mention the chapter ending with this fleeing party of five having a run-in with one of the jolliest, magnificent, and serious characters in history, Father Christmas. In the midst of tragedy, in that darkest hour before sunrise, a lighthearted hope again amplifies in the pages of *The Lion, the Witch and the Wardrobe*.

In the unlikeliest of creatures, a she-beaver, Lewis brings back a much-needed sense of gaiety. During a moment of heartbreak and need of hasty flight for this party, this old she-beaver uses a rather casual logic to help convince the others that there are necessities to pack before they can flee for their lives. Her reasoning is difficult to argue with, though the reader can sympathize with the others' constant beckoning to move more quickly. The whole scene puts the reader on an anxious edge, without forgetting to also make an enjoyable moment through the light quarreling. Lewis crafted this scene so that by the end of the chapter, when Mrs. Beaver is authentically concerned about her sowing machine (for no good, logical reason), a smirk of joy, and not a tear of despair, overtakes the reader's face.

As the five journey into the night, all gaiety disappears for a time. In their tiring journey, there is a beauty that cannot be dismissed, but this beauty is not enough to keep hopes high in the cold night. As the five trek a long path through a difficult night, they have little more than hope of reaching a secret hideout. They have just enough faith that Fortune will favor them. Once they reach the special hiding place, Mrs. Beaver again brings back a bit of mirth with her comment about packing pillows. Then the weariness of the night's hike takes over.

Next morning, rising from an uncomfortable sleep, the five are given a very unexpected boost. Starting with despair and fear when they hear the jingling of oncoming bells, the scene suddenly turns to one of the novel's greatest moments of joy. Mr. Beaver goes topside to see what is actually occurring. The others wait in worry. Then, Mr. Beaver shouts with the sound of good news. What they see as they crawl out into the light is the surest sign that Aslan is on the move, and that the Witch's rule is dissolving: Father Christmas's sledge, and on it Father Christmas himself.

Father Christmas's arrival sets a nice tone of merriment that marries well with the serious nature of the five's current situation. Since the children stepped foot into Mr. Tumnus's cave, they have faced trouble upon trouble, with no real break: one despairing instance after another has rolled over them like a sea full of rogue waves. Since the Beavers have chosen to help the children, they have found nothing but what seems like misfortune. Yet here they stand, Father Christmas himself in front of them, receiving gifts to prepare them for the difficulties ahead, reminding them that there is a real hope of victory, and showing them that good fortune lies ahead, no matter how rough the journey becomes. Joy is on the move in Narnia again and, though war must soon commence, the Witch is losing already.

Without a doubt, Jesus said it best, "... wide is the gate and broad is the road that leads to destruction ... small is the gate and narrow the road that leads to life."[1] The hard truth of this statement has echoed through the centuries, for all who read it or hear it know it to be true. Nevertheless, because of its original context, there is a good point that is not mentioned in Jesus's words from *The Gospel of Matthew*—the road to destruction is often a shorter road than the one to life. I think this is because, since the fall in Eden, mankind has been adrift in an ocean of destruction. Its roaring waves ever crash against our lifeboat, casting salty spray into our eyes with a haunting sting. Each swell tosses a little more destruction over the boat's rim into our lives. We cannot escape its presence. While that life that Jesus speaks of, on the other hand, is like a sun fixed just beyond the horizon. We often feel it pop in with characters of joy, like Mrs. Beaver; we can always see its rays shinning, reflected in that childish longing for Christmas morning; and we can feel its Jovial warmth, even when we do not want to acknowledge it. Still, no matter how far we sail, we cannot cross that horizon's gap. This sun can only be truly reached when the voyage of life is finished and the One who has the authority to bridge the gap takes hold of the sinking lifeboat, carrying it across the expanse.

---

1. Mt 7:13-14 KJV.

11
Sweetly Growing Guilt

Deception for Deception

Dry and tasteless is the hard-earned bread
Of treachery and treason, of guilt and despair.
Deceived for delight, but you'll find instead,
You've been deceived with unliving bread.

The water is cold in this icy place:
Cold as your soul and pale as your face.
No warmth will be gave to the guilty weight
Hung round your neck and sealing your fate.

Don't cry and bemoan the crumbs on your plate;
You've earned every morsel of mold you've ate.
This is the rule you've grossed—don't complain.
Cold is the crown in your dark domain.

Sweetly Growing Guilt

      Sorrow can be so bittersweet,
      For sorrow can make you grow.
      Guilt can bring awakening,
      For on guilt repentance is built.

Sympathy like symphonies,
Drumming and thrumming,
Singing and humming,
Comes rushing with winds
And tingling with brass,
A tune of the blues
That suddenly casts
Itself on the selfish
So they can see past
Their own miseries
And repent of their past.

            The past melts away,
            Like winter in spring,
            When the chick of guilt chirps
            And sorrow's bird sings.
            Turn from your hate
            And you'll celebrate
            With the free-born slave
            Again breaking chains
            With Jubilee's feast—
            Rejoicing with pudding,
            Dinning and chiming.

      Joy is free and ever so sweet.
      Forgiveness brings awakening.
      One is the shoot. One is the root.
      Yet both make the tree.

The Thaw

Come alive! Come alive from root to the sky.
Beneath earthen crust and glaciered-tundra,
Rise. Yes, rise. Grow ever high.
Rise butcher's broom, cast out the dust
Of Winter's Queen. Release Cornwall's heath.
Rise clover and gorse, spring evergreen.
As Ice's reign melts and Sun's fire buds,
When drip turns to flow and flow turns to flood,
As fearless young voices dare overcome,
Life is restored to centuries dead hum.
Flow away! Flow away from tilt to pour.
Flow free from the feet of Bodmin's Moor;
Flow swift through the valley; flow evermore.
Quick, without pause, burrow a gorge
Straight through the plans of Winter's Queen.
Now birds! Now bees!—buzz, flap, sing.
Blue breaks on blue, while the primrose rings.

Reaping What is Sown

When caught up in selfish pursuits, no matter how obvious it may be to us that what we are doing is wrong and what we are involved in will likely end badly, it seems to me that we are still surprised when we reap what we sow. Do we really think, as we slowly reach toward that hot pan sitting on top of the stove to grab that longed for brownie, that we will not be burned? And yet, as soon as our nervous system sends that signal to our brain—"You are burning your thumb!"—we yell out in pain while jumping back with utter surprise. Such foolishness must be hardwired in us from birth. Every time our parents said, "Stop! You're going to hurt yourself," we kept going until we fell on our face. Edmund's deal with the White Queen is no different.

Standing in the Queen's throne room, even after being scolded by the Queen and frightened into giving up information concerning his own family, Edmund's pursuit of Turkish Delight still blinds him from his damned position. He has sown betrayal and is about to reap that betrayal in the fullest. Yet, the burning shock does not hit him until, instead of the princely dish of Turkish Delight, he is given the common food of condemned prisoners, stale bread. Of course, Edmund refuses initially. He refuses until he realizes that if he does not want to be further burned by this situation he has sown and reaped (if he does not want to be killed), he had better be thankful he has only been minorly scalded for his foolishness.

On the sledge ride that follows, Edmund is drug through a long, weary, uncomfortable night. With eyes only on himself, Edmund continues to bemoan his well-earned situation. He is not concerned about what will occur if his current party catches up with his siblings and the Beavers. He only thinks of his family because he knows they would comfort him in this nightmare. He is not concerned with what will come of Narnia if his foolishness turns into good fortune for the Witch. However, despite being buried in this selfish state, a change begins to come—in the frozen world surrounding Edmund, as well as in his frozen heart.

Much to the Witch's dismay, as the morning springs from behind the trees, she discovers a little group of various beasts sitting at breakfast. This breakfast scene would not be so curious and disgusting to the Witch if it were not for the character of the meal. With the various beasts are various dishes, a serious overindulgence in the eyes of this Queen, set out as if to celebrate. What could there possibly be to celebrate in the midst of eternal servitude, fear, and winter? Where could such dishes be derived in a land that is purposefully oppressed to keep out the merriment that such a meal provides? The answer is, of course, that Aslan is really on the move. A fact that the Witch becomes fully aware of when the creatures admit that Father Christmas is the one who supplied the means of their merry meal.

While watching the pathetic scene unfold, something begins to unfold in Edmund, sympathy. Rage overcomes the Saturnine Witch when she can no longer deny the presence of Joy returning to her realm. Wand at the ready, she raises to strike. Edmund cries for her to halt. She does not; they turn to stone. And as the thaw begins to overtake Edmund's heart, so the thaw begins to overtake Narnia.

Leaving the wretched stone figures behind, the sledge goes on, but not for long. Drip falls upon drip until rivers flow freely. Summer skips right past the slow resurrection of spring. Soon, the sledge can no longer be pulled or pushed. In spite of the icy seed the Witch believes to have been perfectly sown and reaped in Narnia over the past century, the Lord of the harvest is causing a new seed to rise in Narnia and Edmund alike, a seed that was sown long before the dawn of time: the seed of redemption.

Edmund has not fully reaped what he has sown, nor has he understood the full price that will need to be paid for his actions. I am not sure he has admitted the greatness of his error to himself or acknowledged the great change that is happening within him. Either way, he has started to think less of himself, and such focus is the beginning of redemption. The only way to undo the harvest of bad seed is to burn it and sow good seed. If Edmund wants to make his redemption complete, he must cast off his foul labor's rotten fruits and sow a different, good seed.

The same goes for us when we are in the midst of a bad situation that we have created with our folly. The longer we dwell on our problem, the problem we have caused, the longer we will dwell in that problem. We reap what we sow. If we want to stop reaping bad fortune, we have to stop sowing bad seed. The first step is taking our eyes off ourselves. Redemption waits.

12
Lion-Hearted Lad

Reaching the Top

Blistered feet, sore with a tough journey,
Find solace in warm, rustling leaves;
The romp of flapping play,
And beating of songbird wings.
Hills and valleys, rocks and plains
Take on forms of the same
Tired wish for journey's-end:
An end that will soon begin
At the top of the last tall hill,
The hardest and most beautiful
To climb.

A King of the Beasts

He stands amongst the crowd—the King, the Beast.
A King of His people—truly humble.
With kindness, love, and friendship for His kin,
With crowds so large they seem to hem Him in,
He calls the beasts and draws their hearts to bow.
The King of all, whose name demands the crowd
To fear, to laugh, to cry. Inside tremble,
Each one who sees His mane—the King of Beasts.

Heavy the hand, heavy the crown that's lain
On those who must look straight into His face.
Who dares to speak to Fear and Good itself?
Who dares to hear the voice that shaped the world?
Only those summoned by heralded fate;
Only those seeking help from His true helm.

Lion-Hearted Lad

Courage is being scared, but not deterred.
Courage steps out into the field prepared
To strike, to fail, to win, to live, to die.
The hero knows the chance is slim, but tries.
He faces noble death without complaint:
Courageously he faces his campaign;
In spite of odds surmounting he will fight
To help the weak and meek preserve their rights.
At bugle's call, at damsel's cry he runs
Headlong into the bout, without question.
So fight and become bane of your own fear.
So strike and kill; yes, pierce the heart and hear
The howl of evil's death that stains the blade
Of charging lines and Lion-hearted lads.
Put knee to dirt, put chin to chest and brace
For regal paws and flat of blade to grace
    Your huffing chest, your humbled breadth's honor.

Courage—Take Hold of Destiny

What could be more satisfying than watching pure evil lose? Watching the innocent rejoice in victory over the schemes of the evil one. Lewis opens this chapter by continuing to focus on the thaw. However, rather than concentrating on this thaw as a loss to the Witch, Lewis shifts the attention to its significance in representing a victory for Lucy, Susan, Peter, and the Beavers. Before this chapter began, these five had roughed it through some serious physical obstacles and spiritual hardships. Now they are finally reaching the end they have been seeking; good fortune is shining with peace and joy. But, this is not their final obstacle in this story, nor is it their final obstacle in this chapter.

Though their way has recently been so blessed that the five have begun to take rest in their journey and even take their current blessings a little for granted, at the top of the last hill, the five will soon be presented with a new, harder challenge. Looking down into the valley below, they see the King they have longed for. And now they must dare to speak to him: the One who is Fear and Good itself—the very voice that shaped the world. This may not seem like a harder challenge than they have recently faced; surely it is more difficult—even a fearful thing—to face Joy itself than it is to flee from evil's bitter grip, for it is in such moments that our own evil is most bare and heavy.

I imagine seeing Aslan for the first time is beyond expression, let alone actually meeting him. How terrifying it must be to stand face to face with one who not only saw the beginning of time and your first breath, but knows every hair on your head—the bad ones included. Ironically enough, maybe the worst part of such a meeting is the moment when you recognize that this One is so magnificent that he would be within his rights to punish you for all your wrong and, instead, he is going to show you undeserved mercy. That being said, I cannot fault the five for their timidity in Aslan's presence. I am sure once the Pevensies stood in front of him, they understood why Mr. Beaver claimed that the Witch would be hard-pressed to even stand in Aslan's sight.

There is a victory in this meeting that needs to be acknowledged. This victory does not come with the defeat of any person. Rather, this victory is over something within one of the Five: Peter's reluctance to take his rightful place. At first, Peter wants to pass off on any other, his right (obligation) to speak to Aslan. Eventually he steps up, which is no small feat. Unbeknownst to Peter, this courageous step leads to a kingship that will soon require more courage to be mustered than he can likely imagine resides in himself at this point. Within minutes of stepping up, Peter is called to yet another battle—the battle that will open his eyes to the kind of heart that really lies just beneath the surface of his boyish skin.

Though it is very difficult to face Joy, it is at least as difficult to stare down certain death in the flesh. It requires just as much lionheartedness to stand before the throne of a king as it does to run headlong into a fight knowing you will likely lose, and the end will be a gruesome death, specifically if this headlong dive is to rescue the weak. Peter's character is uncovered in the moment that he sees Maugrim chomping at Susan's feet. He is not deterred by death. He is afraid, sure—courageous men are afraid. He must move in for the kill anyway. He must be the help. He must be the hero. He is the king. Every piece of the puzzle that makes up his life, every portion of the road that has led to this moment, every battle lost and won in his heart and with his fists up till now has prepared him to earn his rightful place as High King.

Myriad stories have been told about the various avenues, wooded paths, boulevards, mountainous climbs, etc. that make up the grand journey of life. Each of these roads come together to map out an individual's life. Each piece of the map has its own ups and downs, lefts and rights, joys and curses, angels and devils. At the end, these various abridged paths have their own victory or defeat: every victory clears the way for a new, often harder path with a new, often harder battle to be won; with every defeat, on the other hand, there is a chance of redemption—until the final corner is turned and life's end is reached.

In a manner similar to how Lewis has authored the life of Peter Pevensie, his siblings, the Beavers, and all Narnia, your life was authored long before the first whimper that burst forth from your lungs after exiting the womb. The map of your life was drawn in the mind of your creator long before you first planted your feet on the starting line: you were a living being in his heart from eternity. There is a destined end for all of us, and there are destined battles between the start and finish. Still, whatever your end is, whatever destiny awaits you, the Author is waiting for you to step up and take hold of it—to earn it.

13
Wintery-Woes Mended

Prophecy

Scrape ... Scrape ... Scrape

I can hear the sound of metal scrape rock.
I can hear the sound of plans being wrought.
I can hear the sound of prophecies stopped.
I can hear the sound.
Scrape ... Scrape ... Scrape

Can a knife slit through the ties of time
Knotted with the Emperor's hand?
Can spilling of blood take back the rhyme
That's spun by the Emperor's span?
Scrape ... Scrape ... Scrape

I can hear the hopes of an evil twist;
I can hear the hopes of a brooding Witch:
I can feel their ropes wrapped round my wrist.
I can hear the hopes.
Scrape ... Scrape ... Scrape

Can silence deafen the song of Joy
Sung by the Emperor's rushing voice?
Can darkness set up a cunning ploy
To blunt the Emperor's splendid story?
Scrape ... Scrape ... Scrape

I can hear the sound of rushing surprise.
I can hear the hopes of rescuers rise.
I can feel the ropes of bondage divide.
I can hear the hope—
Safe . . . Safe . . . Safe

I can hear the sound
Of righteous rescue romping around.
No longer will I choose to be bound
By delightful tricks and scheming Witch,
By longings in my own heart to twist
A nasty rope of hate that divides
The family knot, long-ago tied
In the Emperor's righteous mind—
The One who fills all prophecy;
The One who will reinstate me.

Wintery-Woes Mended

Secrets spoken, from Self to Savior,
Silently kept and carefully covered
By peaceful arms, in paws of patience.
Potent words, wiping away woes,
Melting guilt's grim and gruesome throes.
Then mended minds, may marry again
With hushed hopes, hoping to hem
Broken bonds, buried beneath sin.
And darn they do, daring to dam
Up ample anger and empty claims.
Newly they notice the narrowed new aim
That excuses the err, extracting the blame.

The Deal

What a sight to behold, a stark contrast to see
The Emperor's Son and the Winter's White Queen:
Helm and the Hangman; the Just to the Cheek,
Discussing the deep sealed beyond all the seas—
    Magic written at dawn in peace.
Not by power nor might can the King take the rights,
Given to the Darkness by the One who is Light,
To take guilty life by the fool's own delight
And place it on stone to slay with a knife.
Is this a wrong; can it be right?
By spirit, the Host, with councils in mind,
Speaks with the Hangman in order to find
A deal to be struck of a grievous kind—
There's only one path that will give respite
    Just long enough to save a life.
As the crowd cheers the news, a question of truth
Arises within the Hangman's longing for proof
Promises will be kept and she will not lose
The rights granted due to treachery's noose.
Will a deafening roar do?

What Consequences May Come

Edmund has chosen to side with the enemy. Soon, that enemy will require his debt of treason against Aslan to be paid; it is her right. For now, however, such rights are not what the Witch is worried about. She is consumed with stamping out any idea that prophecies made against her reign can stand. For victory's sake, the Witch seeks to take Edmund's life, though it means she will not be able to do it properly—she will not be able to kill him on the Stone Table. Edmund has earned judgment from her hand, but she is willing to give that up as long as it suits her current need. As Edmund's treason has a consequence attached to it, so the Witch's attempt to cast off her right will have a consequence.

Enemies like the Witch are concerned about rights when it is beneficial. Such enemies are willing to cast them aside in time of need. Can we fault them for such desires? Everyone wants to discuss rights when it benefits them. Not many want to debate such things when they know it will not work in their favor. Actions and consequences and debts are ever on the lips of those who stand to come out on top. Such things are often swept under the table when circumstances will work the other way around. That is one of the great differences between Aslan and the Witch. Those who are righteous will follow through with the Emperor's commands no matter the cost, while the unrighteous only seek it if it will rule in their favor. The Jovial King's heart is set on merciful obedience, and the Saturnine Witch's on self-preservation.

The Witch truly thinks that a knife can cutout prophecies concerning the Emperor's will. She is foolish enough to believe that she can cheat fate. None can do this. Edmund cannot escape his future kingship, and she cannot escape defeat. They have chosen these paths in the Emperor's mind long ago. As Edmund's treason leads to his physical and spiritual rescue, the Witch's winter leads to her defeat. She has played into the will of the Emperor without realizing it—no other will can be played into but his. The conquering of winter and the forgiveness of the traitor was written into Narnia's story before the Witch's reign, and Edmund's treason was etched into history's pages. Such things were written in the stars before the coalescing of the world. Edmund's every sin and her every move only fulfill prophecy. The Witch cannot see this.

Once Edmund is rescued from the Witch's grasp, and he is securely brought to Aslan's camp, a secret conversation takes place—the first of two secret conversations in this chapter. The reader, along with the other Pevensie children, is not privy to what transpires between Aslan and the traitorous boy. All we know is from that moment forward, Edmund is a different kind of boy. He is guilty and deserves death; I think he knows this now. From the type of character that Edmund displays through the rest of the chapter, I think it is safe to say that his redemption was sealed in his conversation with Aslan. We are not told this explicitly because redemption is a private thing between Savior and Saved. Still, the change that comes to his character is just as drastic as the change that has come upon the landscape throughout Narnia in the last couple days.

When the Witch comes to claim his life, Edmund does not even flinch. Edmund seems to contently radiate a character of faith. No longer does Edmund try to work out his own will or seek his own delight. No longer do arrogance and downright beastliness govern his actions. He appears to trust that no matter what happens, Aslan will see him through. He does not need to plead his own case. He does not need to justify his actions. This kind of faithfulness is always rewarded. It is an ever-fixed hedge around the faithful.

The second secret conversation does not end up being so secret for the reader or Lucy and Susan. The Witch comes to claim her right. The King cannot deny it. The Narnians cannot imagine Edmund being given up and losing their hope of a filled prophecy. Something must be done. Laws have been written since the dawn of time that cannot be backed out on. All treason has a price. Death is the reward of those who side with evil. A debt is owed. What can be done? The secret conversation reveals something to the Witch that is too good to be true. The debt will be paid with a price that will more than suffice, with a price that is worth more than a thousand traitors. But for now, the secret remains.

Time passes over every decision we make so quickly that we neglect to take certain important truisms seriously: actions have consequences; decisions have repercussions; there is a price to be paid for sin; there is a reward for faithfulness. Days pile upon days, turning into years, and these truths often tick by unnoticed, neglected like a clock's perpetually circling secondhand, until it is too late. These truths cannot be ignored forever, for they are, like gravity, unavoidable laws written into the universe; however, they are different than such a law as gravity in this, they are not laws which rely on the existence of the universe—their foundations exist before such physical measurements as time. Moreover, although these truths are strikingly similar to Newton's law of motion, they cannot be measured or scientifically tested. Their truth is not needed to be measured to be known; they are commonly felt and experienced by mankind.

Just like what will come of Edmund's actions, in the end, all we do has consequences; all sin has a price that must be paid. None are safe from the ravages of time without the rescue of time's King. If we do not want to stand in debt when judgment is passed on the laws we have broken, a price must be paid. The King alone has the means to pay for sins committed under Father Time's watchful eye. He alone has the authority to Passover sins previously committed. Be assured, sooner or later, sin catches up with all, and sin requires retribution within the span of time. Once time is played out, the last judgment is passed. Seek, hope, pray, and groan for rescue; it will come, even if only at time's dusk.

14

Guilt, Fortunately Forgiven

Death's Distraction

Concealed underneath a mountain of concern
Lies the crust. Continue digging and discern
That mantle between what the eyes can see
And the soul truly feels—the core's plea—
"A world falling apart: this is a man dying."
Death begins long before that forsaken gasp,
When shoulders drop and hopes lapse;
Concealed between a rock and hard place,
Distraction looms over the condemned's face.
He knows what is coming and must wait.
Here, no promises can be kept or made.
Here, Life must let Death have its play.
Here, Silence will be allowed to overtake.
Dusk is settling on the Dayspring's reign:
Night is descending on His honorable plane:
Red streaks across the end of His last day:
And spirals that ever-red-eye like a flame
On the redemptive shore of Joy's bay.
Still, death does not have the last word.
Morning will come and refuse to be unheard.

Via Dolorosa

It starts. Conviction cuts a path of pain,
A wordless burden bearing down the strong.
His weakness speaks: His face's countenance wanes.
Consoling meek, like mothers, follow along

To help the weakened King to bear the load,
To wipe his face and clear the tears away.
The path's affliction bears again—He folds
To longings pure, for laughing ladies to pray.

At last, with final hill in sight, He falls
For love's sorrowful call: He's shorn and bare
With piercing cares that words can't speak at all.
To sacrifice His all, His final air,

He breathes His last. Descending, now He comes
To be among the rich in death, entombed.

Guilt, Fortunately Forgiven

Floating,
  Slowly swaying
    In the wind, alighting.
      Snipping, snipping away
        At the locks of His beautiful mane.
          Laughing, snarling, bewitched beasts
            Who with trembling cowardice feast,
          In jeering hate, on the bound King.
        Watch as their leader flings
      Back the knife of debt
    To be paid on death.
  Gasping a last breath;
Breathe out forgiveness.
  Evil hags and ogres cheer:
    Finally fortune has steered
      In favor of their doomed career;
        Or so they seem to foolishly think.
          But soon the winds will blow with fate.
        In favor of their favored foes:
      From their own hand befalls
    The deathblow of their cause;
  Not seeing deeper in time
To the deeper rhyme.
  In their hasty, cruel glee
    They will be triumphantly
      Overcome by the shaven King,
        Bound with odious ties unseen.
          For by their stone table and blade,
        A new and living way they've made.
      Guilt is melting, melting away;
    Drying up the shame
  With His mane.

Aslan is Christ

Stop. Think for a minute. You have just witnessed a great feat of humility beyond what most can comprehend. A sacrifice of this magnitude does not come about every day. As a matter of fact, such a sacrifice as you have just witnessed in Narnia can only happen once . . . Well, once in each world. What I mean is this, for every possible world, there is a new possible need for redemption and, at this moment in Narnia's history, redemption was needed. Moreover, the reason such sacrifice and redemption is limited to one per world is there is only one who can make the necessary sacrifice, pay the high price required to redeem souls, worlds, and all fallen things: Jesus Christ, the Son of God.

It is the conscious, and sometimes sub-conscious, recognition of the price required for redemption that leads to the general misconceptions that this work, as well as Ward's *Planet Narnia*, attempt to clear up concerning what exactly *The Lion, the Witch and the Wardrobe* is and who Aslan is. This recognition begs the question, how can Aslan make this sacrifice? Many would answer this in a simplistic fashion: Aslan is Lewis's revision of Jesus, and Aslan's sacrifice is naturally part of this revision. This thought is where the death of Aslan actually loses its power, and the light of Jove (Jupiter) in this tale is drawn away.

In this most famous chapter from *The Lion, the Witch and the Wardrobe*, Lewis delivers a powerful scene that is more than an echo of the Way to the Cross that occurred in our world nearly two-thousand years ago. It may take some by surprise, but Lewis did not write this well-known episode of sacrifice as a mirror to reflect the sacrifice of Christ on Calvary. Of course, this moment of rescue for the traitor (Edmund) reminds us of our own atonement. Of course, we cannot help but watch the harrowing scene and reflect on what is called by many, the Passion of the Christ. Nevertheless, when penning this episode, Lewis was not attempting to just remind us of our own salvific history; he is revealing to us something that is inherent in the nature of the Son of God: self-sacrifice for the salvation of the unworthy. So, what does this mean for Aslan? If he is not a reflection of Christ, who is he?

If there were ever a doubt, before this moment, about Aslan being more than some Christ figure or some allegorical take on what Jesus might be like in another world or story, this is the scene. Aslan is not just some fantastical Narnian version of Jesus. Lewis did not write Aslan to be understood as some type of hypothetical metaphor, some kind of shadow of Scripture. Stop. Think about it for a minute. If Aslan is not a mere reimagining of Jesus, who is he? The answer to this question will draw your eyes back to Enjoy the light Lewis is shining. Aslan IS Jesus in Narnia. Not a new or different kind of Jesus; in Narnia, a world completely different and separate in origin from our own, Aslan is the name which the Son is known by, and lion is the image that he takes own. Still, Aslan IS none other than Christ in Narnia.

We are not told the specifics of how it works; still, that does not change that Lewis reveals Aslan to be incarnate. He, like Jesus in our world, is very much a beast like those he rules over. Not a beast in the nasty, dirty, hateful sense: a beast in the sense that he feels sorrow and abandon, like his people; he knows the tragedy that accompanies love, just like his people; he is subject to death, like his people. Aslan can empathize with those who serve him, those he came to serve.

Though there are parts of this chapter that do lead our minds to think on what was done for us in our own history, this is a new history concerning a new salvation in a new world. For example, Christ was distraught about his destiny in the Garden of Gethsemane, so Aslan is distraught during his night-trek from the Fords of Beruna to the Stone Table. We can clearly see the connection. However, this scene is not a replica. It stands on its own, with its own pain, grief, and humility. The connection we see is not in the story alone. The connection we see, what really makes us think about the similar biblical account, is the character of the one who is giving themselves to save their betrayer.

This is not a reworking of a historical instance from our world in another world. If we are not willing to experience this chapter as a new Passion, in a world completely separate from our own, we will miss its full power. The mocking of Aslan is a fresh ridicule of the Son of God—the Son of the Emperor over the Sea. The hate is new. The evil is new. The Love of God that is willing to trade places with a traitor is the same, for he is the same, no matter when and no matter where and no matter what.

When the hags, ogres, and other foul beasts tie up this humbled king, it certainly brings back images of Calvary's nails. When the Witch plunges the stone blade into Aslan's side, it, in fact, likely calls back to memory the spear in Christ's side. Make no mistake; we can see a story of redemption playing out that is very similar to the one that exists in our own world. The reason for this is not because we are seeing the Passion being reimagined with symbolic creatures. The similarities are not in the images; they are in the main person: Aslan—Christ. The reason we feel so close to this part of the story, and it impacts us so hard, is not because it calls us to think about the past; in a way, we are watching Christ be sacrificed anew. We see and feel the connection to Calvary because, as in our world, in Narnia, Aslan is dying in the stead of a guilty enemy. And in death, he will allow his enemy to be his friend. The only way *The Lion, the Witch and the Wardrobe* can be properly Enjoyed is by not trying to force biblical allusions where they do not belong. The power of Lewis's tale is in recognizing this, Aslan is Christ.

15

Romp . . . Roll . . . Rejoice

Weeping May Endure for a Night[1]

A chill, damp night that chatters the bones—
So pervasive it quivers heart, strength, soul.
As the night moves slow, isolation grows
A loneliness that rivals the deepest heavens;
But within this muzzled hope, something happens.

Scampering through the wet, near-dawn dew,
A seemingly mischievous colony peruses
The miserable scene of spite-tightened ropes;
Then, with nibbling and chewing, make short work.

Weeping—yes weeping, till even tears run dry.
Weeping that endures through the soul's dark night.
Weeping that forgets what comes with sunrise:

His Morning Star, which chases the mourning away;
His joyful heart, which will vanquish this valley.

"Joy cometh in the morning."[2]

---

1. Ps 30:5 KJV.
2. Ibid.

Resurrection: Time's Backward Aim

Come "Dayspring from on high;"[3] come with the new sunrise.
Come King and Ruler, you must deliver.
Come with Angelic hosts, rising over the coasts
With crystalline song, you have done no wrong.
Come crack the stone in two; with an echoing boom,
Come king—come kingly. Come boasting, beaming
With a voice that rumbles, and footsteps that crumble
Treachery's fair claim with time's backward aim—
Turn back! Turn back! Turn back before the dawn, in fact.
And there you will find the hands that turn time.
And there you can release time's captives from their place.
And there you can turn the wheel that has spurned.
And with innocent blood, turn back the current's flood
To before the dawn, where the magic spawned;
Then grant with the new dawn a magic from beyond,
Magic from before this continued war.
Come victory, come charge the front lines with a surge
Of glorious boast: the nightfall has lost.

---

3. Lk 1:78 KJV

Romp . . . Roll . . . Rejoice

Romp . . . Roll . . . Rejoice.
Strength restores with a rolling voice.
Smile . . . Spin . . . Shout.
Bliss bursts in like a spinning spout.
Laugh . . . Love . . . Leap.
Life breaks out, putting death to sleep.
Frolic . . . Flip . . . Fall.
The chase ensues with loving calls,
Through meadowy mirth and green spring,
Pouncing about with offerings
Of praiseful cheer with the true King.

But celebration must cease.
Now mount up, ride swiftly.
Quick, set the captives free—
Move faster than derby-speed.

Bound high above barriers,
Let nothing stop your task.
With radiant drive,
Destroy the cast.

That Day that is Deeper than Time

Losing someone who is dear to us is one of those tragic experiences that most mankind shares in common. In my opinion, the only commonly shared experience that is more tragic is being there to witness the moment when life slips from their face; it is like watching their whole life disappear in a single exhale of breath that never retracts. There is but a single word that can describe what it feels like when you look into their expressionless face, disbelief. The surrounding world keeps spinning, while your heart, soul, and mind remain frozen in disbelief. Weeping fades into blank stares as your mind attempts to convince your heart, "This is really happening." If you have ever experienced this, then you can likely comprehend that state of despair that Lucy and Susan are in as they stare at Aslan's lifeless face. The only comfort that can even begin to crack through the darkness in such a moment is the Christian's faithful hope, "Death does not have the last word"—Joy always returns, and Joy inevitably triumphs.

Lewis crafts the beginning of this chapter in such a way that the reader can feel Lucy and Susan's heartache. The kisses, strokes, and cries paid as homage to this holy, slain beast are written in a manner that wrenches the reader's own heart. The confusion that overwhelms them is not just understandable, it is to be expected. Time's seemingly slow progression, prolonging the unbelievable reality lying next to them, certainly draws back memories of such long nights for readers who have shared this pain.

Common to such situations, a scampering, seemingly insignificant hope appears to offer a bit of comfort. Mice appear from the tall grass and begin to chew at the ropes. In the moment, such attempts at bringing hope are cast off by the distraught as nothing more than a trifle in comparison to the pointlessness of chewing through the bonds. Proven here, and in many instances like it, this attitude is misguided. Given enough time, that helping hand or attempt at encouragement that appears to be useless while under the duress of sorrow will prove not to have been in vain.

As they pace back and forth in the early morning, merely to keep warm and, without a doubt, to try and look past the awful occasion, Lucy and Susan are taken aback by a loud noise. The Stone Table has cracked in two, and Aslan is no longer bound on top of it. Like at the resurrection of Christ, the ladies are confused; they think someone has taken the body. Suddenly this confusion is set straight. The "Dayspring from on high"[4] has come with the new sunrise. A deeper magic has been called on. Time's backward aim has been enacted. Aslan's love and faithfulness have fulfilled the very aim of the Emperor's magic (law), vanquishing dark magic (lawlessness).

The time has come for something new. A new day has dawned. A new era has dawned. It is time to break the evil spell that the Witch has put over Narnia and its inhabitants. But first, a celebration is in order.

I often wonder why characters like Aslan never seem to be in a hurry. In the fast pace world we live in, I sometimes get anxious watching the romp and revel that occurs in scenes like the one between the newly resurrected Aslan and the Pevensie girls. Why in the world are they prancing and frolicking and not getting to work? I have come to realize that such questions come from a true blindness: we cannot see the world from God's perspective. There is a time for everything, and everything works in God's time. There may be a time for celebration in the middle of war. There may be a time to rejoice on the edge of battle. We must, as Aslan and the girls do, see and take advantage of these times. Whether facing common, daily hardship or some once in a lifetime, catastrophic peril beyond imagining, before stepping onto the field of battle, we should remind ourselves why we bother to struggle: Joy.

Once in the right mindset, meaning once the Pevensie sisters have again begun to look along good fortune, they hop onto Aslan's back and ride for the Witch's castle. After the gallop is over, they pounce over the wall so that they may now melt away the seemingly bad fortune which has befallen the stone figures in the Witch's court and recruit an army to destroy her power forever.

4. Ibid.

THAT DAY THAT IS DEEPER THAN TIME

The mourning that opened the chapter has grown into rejoicing—time itself turned back the effect of its hands and brought rejoicing with a new morning. Some days, life opens with mourning. Some days present us with a loss that seems too difficult to bear. Those days will drag on. Those days will be full of misery. No words will take away the pain; it would be wrong not to allow ourselves or others to feel the pain. In our fallen world, pain is a natural part of love. Lucy and Susan love Aslan; that is why they are distraught when he dies. Mourning is real, and we must all face it without forgetting that rejoicing is real too. Even in the blackest night, we can be assured that the sun will rise again. When it does, we can revel in its warmth and beauty. Then we will have the courage to breathe life into all those souls frozen in grief; we will be able to call them to join with us in looking at and along its light to see the victory that lies ahead; and at that final day we will, with the Lord of Time, call Father Time to turn back his hand on the sorrows of loss—we will rise in that land, on that day that is deeper than time.

16

Heroic Helm of Nations

Breathe Life—Prepare for Battle

Gentle exhalation of warm breath
Igniting the inner-beast.
Ripening beams of Kingly spirit
Setting the sleeper free.
Row upon row, luft after luft,
The dead court, enlivening.
Here. There. Uphere. Overthere.

Then, neither last nor least,
That startling lamp-post friend,
That little red-clad gent,
That once sided with the foe,
But now the greatest friend,
Inhales the gentle, Kingly blow.
Now captivity ends.

From toe to nose, awaken the might
Of bumbling stature.
Breathe magic, bring back life
In this Fee-fi statue.
Fo-fum—let him swing his club
And sack this castle.
Partitions break and towers crash—

Off to find the battle.
With gladness, this merry band gathers
To check the queen.
With magnanimity, the troops march
To set their land free.

Leonine Pride

    Pick up the trail. Sniff out the scent.
    Ride for the fight; prepare to rent

The enemy lines with Leonine banner.
Carry the weight of friendship's banter.

    Move out in waves. Trot on in pairs.
    Together, face down this dangerous affair.

Run ready with haste, that Leonine stride—
Laughing with faith; growling with pride.

    March on, justice! Stamp on, empire!
    Quicker, faster, let burn that fire

Raging inside your Leonine drive.
Frenzied, attack and protect the hive.

    Sharpen your wits. Steady your hands.
    Pounce over hills in brotherly bands.

Break on the ranks with Leonine power.
Rejoice in the bout with ancestral valor.

Swift, Sound Judgement

The battle resounds.
The howling of hounds
The fighting, it still ensues.

The swinging of blades.
The price being paid.
The many take on the few.

The fallen, filled ford.
The friendly armed hoard
The battlefront is defused.

The blink of an eye.
The King passes by.
The accuser stands accused.

The King overcomes.
The accuser is judged.
The enemy is removed.

Friendship-Love

Those who are familiar with Lewis's philosophical works have likely come across his thoughts on love in his book *The Four Loves*. If not, it is a must-read. But for those who are not much for reading nonfiction, I will suggest that you get a copy of Lewis's *Till We Have Faces*: a fantastic, fictional reworking of the Cupid and Psyche myth. Not only is this story of love a favorite of many Lewis fans, it was Lewis's favorite. Throughout this book, Lewis has mainly focused on two of these loves: family and friendship. (Of course, as in the story of our world, God-love undergirds the whole story for God is omnipresent.) Early on in the book, familial-love is the story's more noticed impetus. During Lucy's first trip to Narnia, however, a new love is introduced as the driving factor, friendship.

Now it is time for those under the Witch's spell to be set free. Their shared torture leads to a shared moment of freedom. Their shared freedom leads to a shared cause, to conquer the Witch. Sometimes friendship is that simple, though no less powerful: we romp and revel with friends; we laugh with friends; we fight with and for friends; and, if nothing else, we are friends with the enemy of our enemy. This ragtag group of various beasts has come to that moment when a shared enemy causes a friendship that defines an entire country's future.

No doubt, one of the most beautiful moments in this chapter is when Tumnus is found and set free. Lucy has been heartbroken for this kind faun ever since she discovered his wrecked home. The love shared between these two jovial friends causes the beginning of numerous hardships; nonetheless, the obstacles that result from their love prove to be the only path to overturning winter's hold on Narnia. Inevitably, their love covers a multitude of sin. Friendship-love is the type of love that people share which makes the struggles of life worth it because it is one of the great sources of Joy. Each struggle faced as a consequence of their love does not lead from despair to despair, though despair does seem quite pervasive until this chapter. Each struggle faced as a consequence of their love leads from victory to victory.

Lewis does not paint the coming battle as a fearful thing. To the recently redeemed, this battle is a gift of Jove. Together, these new friends march to defeat the evil one. Conquering that evil will further forge their shared citizenship in Narnia and strengthen their friendship as loyalists to the cause for freedom. They are marching against the cold, slow progress of a teetotaler-Witch. They are marching to set all Narnia free from the Saturnine captivity of misery. This march is not one of reservation with an overshadowing gloom. This march is one of hearts filled with galloping gallantry and mouths bursting with brotherly banter. The struggle that this group is about to facedown is not feared at all; it is looked forward to as a time when those marching can give grace for the grace they have received—they are marching for friendship's sake. This march of friends for Narnia ends with a most glorious sight, terror in the Witch's face as she realizes that death was no match for the truest friend of Narnia.

Life is a struggle. Daily we are confronted with various obstacles, both new and ongoing. Yet for some reason, we press on. Some may be pessimistic and say we press on in the mire because we know no other way: we find ways to cope with reality because we desire to survive; survival instincts are the only force that keep us evolving, or at least surviving; that is all that life really is, the propagation of the species. To ones such as these, friendship is just a survival tool. (I say poppycock!) Others, however, may have an optimistic outlook. Such individuals may say we press on through the deep waters and thick mud because, whether or not we survive, the best parts of life are forged there; once such obstructions are pushed through, the best parts of life will be found stronger on the other side. To ones such as these, friendship is not a means to an end but a blessing that gives meaning to the beginning, middle, and end.

Friendship is more than surviving and deeper than instinct. Friendship is not evolutionary: friendship is beyond evolution; friendship is beyond progress; friendship is one of those best parts of life that gives a reason to progress, and it is the progress sorely needed in our lives and culture. From the beginning, friendship has been one of those things which have kept men fighting and dying for each other, even against the logical, evolutionary-progress (as some men have seen it) of humankind. This fighting has not been endured because men know no other way. This dying has not continued to save the fittest. Like the friends of Aslan at the Battle of Beruna, this fighting has endured because conquering evil is the only way to Joy. This dying has been endured to save all, especially the helpless. That is the heroic way of friendship-love.

17

Returning With Wishful Wonder

Beautiful, Wonderful, Lovely

What could be more beautiful?
What could be more fraying
Than watching the penitentful
Heart of the traitor obeying
His savior's call to selfless love?
—a cost worth repaying.

What could be more wonderful?
What could be more touching
Than the pierced hand's merciful
And passionate act of healing
Their betrayer's death-wounds?
—a cost that's worth paying.

>Still, there is more work to be done.
>The contrite heart is not the only one
>In need of saving—in need of healing.
>And their wounds, too, are beautiful.
>And their healing, too, is wonderful.
>And their sacrifice, too, is lovely.

What could be more lovely?
What could be more telling
Than a prince, knighted meekly
On the field of battle, kneeling
Before his secret savior?
—the reason for paying.

What could be more beautiful?
What could be more lovely
Than brethren dwelling together,
Than brethren fighting together,
Than brethren living together,
Than brethren dying together
In unity?

Enthroned

The   Lesser   Court.
This   Gallant   Fort.
Once.   Always.   Ever.
Crown the Magnificent
And the Gentle!
Crown the Just
And the Valiant!
In halls of masonry
And rooms of feathers
Adorned with many colors;
Yet, ever under the helm of another.

Under roofs of ivory
And vaulted ceilings,
Beneath great spires
And stained-glass-light,
Anoint the thrones
And crowns with weeping.
Rejoice with Mer-songs
And glorious sights
Of worlds uniting
And revelry flowing,
Of courtly dancing
At vigorous heights.
Reward the heroes
And honor their help
With cords of grace
And smiling face.
With scepter in hand,
Remember the ends
Of their sacrifice
And honor that price.

The   Lesser   Court.
This   Gallant   Fort.
Once.   Always.   Ever.
Praise the Magnificent
And the Gentle!
Praise the Just
And the Valiant!
In the midst of said praise,
Let the Untame-One slip away.
Yes, let Him return when He may;
Ever rejoice until that day, until that age.

Returning with Wishful Wonder

Return, Pure Coat, without blemish or spot.
O Wish Giver, grant yourself to be caught.

Through thickets, then thinly, undergrown brush,
Lead on the hunt that will lead to the quest—
Lead on the chase that will lead on to change.

Bring back memories from forgotten days.
Step after step, in pursuit of a wish.
Wondrous Stag, is this change the gift?

Return without coats, fall back through the door
Where adventure began and will no more
Be a way to great quests and earned valor.

But, if you should meet any like visitors,
Who have themselves fallen through a strange door,
You may share your tale of transcendent lore.

And rest in the chance it will come again.
When you're not looking and least expect, then
Zap! You'll be back among the Narnians.

Anxious one, while you wait, remember this . . .
The Wondrous White Stag led you here as a gift,
And will lead you back when His time permits.

Looking Along Life

When reading a book, it is easy to recognize that nothing happens by chance. A good author always makes sure to give their readers a chance to see certain events coming. Beginning in grade school, we learn about literary techniques like foreshadowing because such knowledge will help us to follow a story's flow. There is no such thing as coincidence. Nothing happens by accident. It was no coincidence that the Pevensie children went to stay at Professor Kirk's house or that a rainy day called for an exploration that led Lucy into a magical wardrobe. It was no coincidence that Lucy and Tumnus were in Lantern Waste at the same time, nor was it an accident that Edmund and the Witch crossed paths. There is a reason the traitor (Edmund) is the one that sacrifices himself on the edge of evil's sword in order to be resuscitated by Lucy's jovial cordial—that gracious gift from Father Christmas. It all happened according to plan. That guiding spirit of the book, sometimes revealed though mostly hidden, led them all the way through: path to path, obstacle to obstacle, faith to faith, and grace to grace. A good author uses their writing chops to send that spirit out to the reader and draw them along as well, to see that neither a single pen-stroke nor ink-blot were scribbled or dribbled by chance.

However, an even better author will leave a certain element—the foundation—unseen and unseeable when properly experiencing the story, for that element which is unseeable is the very light the reader looks along to see all the other typical literary techniques. Lewis is undoubtedly one of those even-better authors. It may seem that things just happened to fall into place at just the right time, and so, when reading the work of a good author, we should expect it to be so. Nothing in a good novel is by chance because the author directed it. But, there is a reason beyond chance and what we are allowed to see that has guided the better author's (Lewis's) pen. There is a secret influence in this story guiding the characters and the reader alike, from start to finish. For even-better authors, *nothing* is by chance, and every play on words, description, and shadow are not just used to show what will unfold in the story but are used to help cause something to unfold in the reader. The secret influence is not only a light to look along the story; it is a light to enlighten the heart and mind of the reader, albeit secretly.

Finally, the last chapter has come. The battle for Narnia has been won. The traitor (Edmund) has crushed the Witch's power. Aslan has killed the Witch. By the middle of the chapter, the Four will sit on the thrones at Cair Paravel; the prophecies will be fulfilled. The Four will be honored and become honorable rulers. Their reign will be long and prosperous. Fortune has smiled on the Pevensies. Fortune has smiled on Narnia. Still, by the end of the chapter, Fortune will reveal further plans in a most fortunate event, the appearance of the White Stag.

In folklore, the White Stag leads its pursuers on a quest that will bring about a change. Lewis foreshadows the coming of the White Stag in the second chapter by speaking of it, via Mr. Tumnus, as a symbol of Narnian prosperity. The reader is set to think that if prosperity comes back to Narnia, so will the White Stag. Moreover, Tumnus reveals that the White Stag is a creature that grants wishes if it is caught. This further signals the reader to keep an eye out for the White Stag; if, likely when, the White Stag comes back into the story, it will be chased—a wish will be sought from this noble creature. So, when the Four hear of the Stags return and begin their hunt, the reader knows a time for change is at hand.

Once the Four are left to themselves in the wood, suspicion grows; something is about to happen. Gradually the Four begin to realize where they are, Lantern Waste, and that they have been there before. They push through the woods. Step after step, things begin to change. The pace of revelation quickens until . . . Woah! Plop! Smack! Aahhh! . . . the Four push through the wardrobe door and find themselves lying on the creaky wooden floor in that old, strange house. They are children again.

A change has happened in the children, and not just physical. A more important change has come. The secret element, the Joviality behind the story's overall development, has transformed the children into helpful heroes of laughter, rulers of deep thought, and lion-hearted lovers of Joy. And if Lewis has successfully implemented the secret element—the influential air, the guiding spirit—by the closing page, the reader too has grown into a more Jovial character than they were when the story began.

Too often we passingly handle life as if it is a set of random events with no general or specific purpose. Many of us only begin to think on the series of unfortunate events in life as part of a bigger plan when we are in need of comfort from the various pains that we have a hard time accepting. Most of the time, it seems as if we do not attribute fortune or misfortune to more than chance—the spin of the wheel. Life is lived quite passively by the masses.

Do not get me wrong, I know some of us do, sometimes, see that occasional glimmer of light that keeps us smiling and know—I mean really know—that there is Someone out there guiding us. In those instances, we can see the play unfolding, and it is glorious. Deep in the inner-man, just for a moment, we catch a glimpse: the Author of the Eternal Play is watching over each character with care; God, the Playwright is working out his masterpiece—this tragicomedy-fairytale. God is writing our story in such a way that, if we learn to look along the light of fortune in our lives, we will be changed into the character that he has created us to be. If we can bring ourselves to acknowledge that there is a secret element at work in our story that we cannot see, and submit to it in good faith, we will be shaped and molded by, and into, that influential air God has placed as the guiding spirit in our story.

Lewis wrote this first published story in his fairytale so that we could look along that Greatest Fortune. He has done his job well; that is why we keep going back to the world he created. Through the light of Narnia, we can see Joy. And as the author of this book, I hope that I have helped the reader of Lewis to stop trying to Contemplate Narnia, and, therein, miss the fullness of Joy. I hope I have, somehow, caused the reader to Enjoy Narnia. (Or, at least I hope I have provided the proper tools.) Further than this, however, I can only pray that Lewis, other great authors like him, and I have somehow helped our readers to look along their own lives—the story that God wrote.

Your life is a story that the Author (God) means you to Enjoy.

Epilogue

Joy Through a Wardrobe

Donegal, London, Paris, Dublin,
Everywhere has a certain air,
An influence and character.

Homes, cities, countries, planets,
There is a spirit lying inherent,
A value its visitors may inherit.

You will feel it and never see it,
Though it looms on, permanent,
Weaving through like fine fabric.

It moves right through, it seeps into,
Ever true, every part of you.
Let Good Fortune's planet move.

Joy, laughter, justice, valor,
Do appear in the atmosphere
Of Good Fortune's Jupiter.

Plant your feet, begin the feast
On words you meet—great to least—
More than verbiage, they do speak.

Quick, go through the old Wardrobe
Into the world woven by Jove—
Follow the bird; lighten your load.

Who can catch this woven bird?
Who can make this spirit burn?
Who can bake this planet's fare?
Who can pen this symbolled air?

>A Jack of many trades.
>A Jack with many friends.
>A Jack who is clever
>With an inkwell and pen.

www.ingramcontent.com/pod-product-compliance
Lightning Source LLC
Chambersburg PA
CBHW070505100426
42743CB00010B/1770